EXCHANGE SETBACKS FOR WINNING

The Secrets To a Prosperous Life

Cynthia Asante

Exchange Setbacks For Winning: The Secrets to A Prosperous Life
Asante, Cynthia

Copyright © 2018 by Cynthia Asante

ISBN: 978-1-9993538-0-3

All rights reserved. No part of this publication may be reproduced, stored in a retrieval system or transmitted in any form or by any means, electronic, mechanical, photocopying, recording, scanning or otherwise.

Although the author and publisher have made every effort to ensure that the information in this book was correct at press time, the author and publisher do not assume and hereby disclaim any liability to any party for any loss, damage, or disruption caused by errors or omissions, whether such errors or omissions result from negligence, accident, or any other cause.

All rights reserved, including the right to reproduce this book or portions thereof in any form whatsoever.

Published by:
10-10-10 Publishing
Markham, Ontario

First 10-10-10 Publishing paperback edition

Contents

Dedication • v
Foreword • vii
Acknowledgements • ix

CHAPTER 1	What Have You Been Told? • 1
CHAPTER 2	Setbacks • 15
CHAPTER 3	Be Aware • 27
CHAPTER 4	The Secret To Your Exchange • 39
CHAPTER 5	Let's Check Out Your Investment • 51
CHAPTER 6	Let People Be Your Inspiration • 69
CHAPTER 7	Invest With The Little You Have • 85
CHAPTER 8	Use Your 5 Senses To Get What You Want • 99
CHAPTER 9	Success Is Predictable • 107
CHAPTER 10	Living Is Giving • 125
CHAPTER 11	Share Your Investment • 139
CHAPTER 12	Stay A Winner • 147
CHAPTER 13	Leave Your Mark • 167

Recap • 177
About the Author • 179

*I dedicate this book to YOU.
It is my deepest desire for you to find
your life purpose and full potential.*

*And to my mother Rebecca,
if it wasn't for you, I wouldn't be the woman I am today.*

Foreword

How do you move away from your setbacks, to live the life you really want? Even with all the resources you have today, this question is difficult to answer.

The main problem with setbacks is that when you go through them, you are very much consumed with your own life and thinking. As a result sometimes you are unable to have a clear mind or discover what you really want. Making sound decisions can be especially difficult during this period. You will at some point experience setbacks in your life.

Whether your setbacks are behind you, or you are experiencing them now, I want you to get your hopes up and position yourself for an extraordinary journey.

Exchange Setbacks for Winning gives specific and simple directions to discover the true potential that is in you. Each and every chapter contains great ideas to help you get closer to your dreams. Author Cynthia Asante shows you how to use any setback to your advantage. This book has all the information you need to live a successful life. What I like the most is the ancient secret that is revealed in this book—to discover your life purpose you will have to turn your focus towards others and look beyond yourself, especially when faced with life challenges.

Cynthia's greatest passion and drive is to help you find your own vision, and leave your own legacy. *Exchange Setbacks for Winning* really lives up to its title. Cynthia's life experience is a captivating story. I am inspired by the honesty and the vulnerability of this book.

I hope the words in this book will not only inspire, encourage and bring you hope, but also have an effect on you as you apply the life-changing principles. Whatever stage you are in, know that by reading

Exchange Setbacks for Winning

this book you will see your personal and professional relationships excel and deepen. You will live a more enjoyable and fulfilled life.
Be blessed and thank you for choosing to develop yourself.

Raymond Aaron
New York Bestselling Author

Acknowledgements

I appreciate YOU. Thank YOU for purchasing this book and working on becoming the best version of you.

I am blessed beyond my own understanding; thank you, **Rebecca Korantema**, for stepping into the mother's role and loving me beyond my wildest dreams. Not once in my lifetime have you ever doubted my dreams but have always cheered me on to pursue my deepest desires. I still hold what you once said, when I asked you how I could ever thank you for the love you give me. You said, "Akua, I want you to do what you are meant to be doing here on earth—fulfill your purpose. I will be the most blessed mother when I see you fulfilling your God-given dream." I love you with all my heart. (Akua is my Ghanian name.)

To **Jacques Asiedu**, for being the greatest father to me, and the best husband to Rebecca. Thank you for all your support and encouragement, and for believing in my dreams, and embracing and loving me as your own flesh and blood.

To the most amazing, fabulous, smart, loving, and generous sister in the world: **Cindy**, thank you for all your support and encouragement throughout every season.

To my brother, **Mike**, for your input and support, and for believing in me and my dreams. I am blessed to have you, and you believe that I can do anything in this world.

To my cousin, **Daniel Adofo-Kyei**, for the meaningful chats in Ghanan, and for our previous holiday in Italy. I always enjoy your company when we spend time together.

And of course, to my cousin, **Bernard**, for support, friendship, and the good late night chats over the phone.

Thank you, **Raymond Aaron** for your insightful ideas, wisdom, and support, and for guiding me in the process of writing this book. What a wonderful opportunity the 10-10-10 program is! You have not only provided me with an abundance of joy and success but have also dramatically impacted my life. I know that my life will never be the same again.

I am extremely grateful for **Dr. Gregory Roberts;** to me, you are the best GP I have ever come across. You have cared for me more than I could ever ask for, and I am blessed that we crossed paths. You were always available for me when I was sick, and even after my recovery—thank you for your commitment and faithfulness to me.

Dr. Ash Hanafy, I deeply appreciate the wisdom you hold, which helped you to save my life. You thought outside the box, and I am inspired by your *big thinking*.

I thank you both, doctors, for treating me like your own daughter, and for doing everything in your power to keep me here. Thank you for extending your love to me and wishing me all that my heart desires.

Life with no guidance is setting yourself up for very minimal or no success at all. I have been amazingly blessed to have coaches and mentors cheering me on over the years. Thanks to you, I can say I am living an extraordinary life.

To **John Scott**, for your ongoing immense support and encouragement, and for believing in my dreams. Thank you for your faithful friendship, your wisdom, and for being in this life with me. I don't have enough words to express how blessed I am to have you and to know that you are always there for me.

To **Leo Lute**, for loving me as your own daughter, and for encouraging me to believe that I can do and become anything I want in this life. You have always believed in me, and have stuck up and fought for me when it counted. From age 16, you have been living this life with me; I am forever indebted.

To **Yvonne Mathews**, for your wisdom, your advice, and your brilliant ideas that helped me write and complete this book. I couldn't wish for anyone else but yourself to guide me through the process of

Acknowledgements

writing this book. You are the best!

To **Wendy Taylor**, for bringing me into your home and creating a peaceful environment for me to work on my private practice, and for supporting me with all the immigration issues.

To **Frankie van den Hoek**, for all your supervision hours and the good times we spend outside the practice room.

To **Raymond Southon**, for teaching me to become an outstanding counsellor and to not see clients as numbers but as individuals, as they are always worth our time.

To **Yvonne Rensink**, for all your support over the years. You have never stopped checking on me, and you made sure I succeeded in pursuing some of my greatest moments in life.

To **Jenny and Ed van Loenen**, for supporting me during my college years in Australia.

You embraced me as your own, made me part of your family, and opened your home to me. I want to express my love and sincere thanks:

To **family Owusu**, **Albert** and **Akua**, for your perfect generosity and care, and for taking me on board as your own daughter. My words on paper could not express how blessed I am with your love.

To **family Goldstine**, **Don** and **Sevda**, for all your love and support, and for helping me out when I need you. **Sevda,** your name says it all; as I always said, you are the true meaning of a best friend. Thank you for being attentive, caring, available, fun, faithful, easygoing, forgiving, and empathetic.

To **family Rehma**, **Tod** and **Lissa**, for your wisdom and guidance, and for believing in my dreams and being great influential figures in my life.

To **family Greenfield**, **Brian** and **Jenny**, for all your support and for cheering me on to pursue what my heart desires. **Jenny**, thank you for being a faithful friend and extending your generosity to me.

To **family Marfo**, **Yaw-Emil** and **Hilda**, for all the value you add to my life, and for the beautiful Christmas times we shared.

To **family Taubert**, **Ryan** and **Primrose**, for being the greatest example of generosity, love, and care that I know; not to mention the many laughs we shared. Thank you for creating good times with me.

To **family Makedonez**, **John** and **Donia**, for bringing me into your home when I needed a place to stay, and for giving me the best 31st birthday party ever!

To **family Athenasio**, **John** and **Ruth**, for all your great advice, your wisdom, and your spiritual guidance in my life. **Ruth**, thank you for editing my thesis during my university years, and for your ongoing encouragement and your love.

To **family Aggrey**, **Lydia** and **Prince**, for your continuous words of encouragement, and for helping me to believe in the impossible.

To **Kofi A. Ameyaw**, for your caring thoughts, love, and support.

To **Anthony** and **Linda Nguy**, for supporting me through my university years, standing with me to pursue some of my dreams, and assisting me with the startup of the private practice in counseling.

To **Rhys** and **Emily Velingos**, for giving me a special room in your house, named after me ;-). You are one of my best friends, who I can trust no matter what season I am in, and you are always there for me when I need you. Thank you for taking care of me during my recovery, and for looking after all my stuff while I was absent.

You made the transition of my life easier, helping me to leave the past behind me; and in exchange, I received hope for the future, with deep appreciation:

To **Jeroen Koopman** and **Regine Mendez**, for all your encouragement during the writing of this book. **Regine**, from the first time I met you, you have been my greatest support, and I could not wish for a better sister's friendship than yours.

To **Vicke** and **Tessa Donker**, for being amazing friends and for helping me out during my high school years. You were there for me during the toughest seasons of my life, and you took me in when I ran away from home. Thank you!

To **Mia** and **Kim Wijnands**, for living this life with me, and for all the good times. **Kim**, my best friend from kindergarten, I love you and thank you for the lifelong friendship.

To **Neil O'Conghaile**, for the tremendous support you provided when I came to Ireland.

Acknowledgements

To **Jessica Kaluwaji**, for believing in me and standing with me through every trial; you are an amazing friend and sister, and I love you.

To **Dickson Osei**, for your unconditional love for me, your ongoing support, and for believing in my dreams.

To **Yodit Jacob**, for a lifelong friendship; I am so proud of you for where you are today. Your unbeatable spirit inspires me; thank you for creating some of the best memories of my life: 2017, in Ireland.

To **Bernise Pektuzun**, for your caring thoughts and love for me. I love your contagious laugh; every minute spent with you is more than a million dollars' worth.

To **Patricia A. Wiafe**, for spoiling me every time I come to your place, and for all your advice and encouragement. You are an incredible woman.

To **Rupert Muir**, for your emotional support during the phase of my illness, and for being by my side.

To **Silvia F,** for your friendship, advice, and wisdom you brought to my life.

To the founders of Kookai Australia, **Robert Cromb** and **Danielle Vagner,** and managers, **Kate Cruisink**, **Naomie M,** and **Sarvi D,** for your support, and for creating opportunities for me during my time at Kookai.

To the amazing, fabulous, crazy and fun Kookai ladies, **Jessica A**, **Ashley Pritchard**, **Ashley M**, **Laura**, **Elissa**, **Katherine**, **Samantha**, **Alicia**, **Chloe**, **Katie H**, **Dani**, **Lauren S**, **Teresa**, **Thalia**, **Candice** and **Chiara**, for the epic and adventurous nights out, and for the quiet nights in. Thank you for keeping my life light and fun; I love you all.

I would like to thank **William Owusu**, **Adjo Quainoo**, **Jun E**, **Jim Q**, **Ilker**, **Rogune**, **Hezel**, **Tracy H**, **Ulrike**, **Sanchala**, and **Nicola T** for sending text messages or calling to check on me, and for loving me unconditionally. **Ada D**, **Kim B,** and **Cassandra G**, thank you for the great and fun times during our college years in Australia; I still hold those beautiful memories.

Hon. **Philip Ruddock,** former MP, and **Jeannette Farrell**, thank you for believing in my dreams, and for providing me with my permanent residency. I am forever grateful for the great and prosperous life you made available to me in Australia.

To Hillsong Church Senior Pastors, **Brian** and **Bobbie Houston,** for your extraordinary leadership; this has not only helped me to become strong in my faith but has also helped me ground myself and become the person I am today. You definitely have impacted my life, and I thank you for that.

To **all** the wonderful **Hillsong Church pastors,** and with special thanks to **Robert Furgesson, Lee** and **Cherie Burns, Mark, Tony, Peter Smith, Nathan Mclean,** for your support, guidance, and teachings. I can never put a price on the spiritual growth and training I experienced under your leadership.

To Liberty Church Senior Pastors, **Noel** and **Sharon Kenny,** for your exceptional love, your encouragement, and your overwhelming support. I am so grateful to be under your leadership, and I couldn't imagine a better one while staying in Ireland.

To **Louice Cassidy,** for believing in my dreams and taking this project further than my imagination. I feel blessed to have you in my life, and I thank you for all your support. I love how you never stop smiling, no matter what life throws at you; you are very inspiring.

I would like to thank **each person who calls Liberty Church,** at Dublin 8, Bray and Clondalkin, **their home,** for your friendship, love, and encouragement during the process of writing this book.

To my beautiful friend, **Leanora Skelly,** you are a strong woman and an inspiration to me; you have overcome every setback, and I have nothing but great admiration and respect for you.

I would like to thank **all my clients** for trusting me with your stories, and also for impacting my life as much as I did yours.

I am honored to be part of the best Creative Writing Group in Dublin. I feel so uplifted, encouraged and inspired, every time we come together. To **Niall B, Sean Condon, Patrick, Frank, Bob, Stephen** and **Sean F, Jett,** and **Ann B,** thank you for all your positive input, and for helping me finish writing this book.

I appreciate everything I have learned from **award winning author, Declan Burke.** Thank you for your coaching tips, your advice,

Acknowledgements

and great ideas that helped me write this book.

To **Sheila Keegan**, for starting the Creative Writing Group, and for inspiring me to think big and to be more creative with my writing.

A warm and special thank you for the awesome, likeminded friends I met on the Momentum 2018 event.

To **George Anderson**, for organizing and hosting an inspiring and motivating event: Momentum. I left the event with new and powerful ideas for my goals.

To **Gerry Duffy**, for giving me the insight and understanding of how we can get distracted by the little things in life. Your illustration with the backpack changed my life for the best.

To **Pat Divilly**, for encouraging me to put dates for my goals and dreams. This helped me to work harder, meet deadlines, and accomplish writing this book.

To **Paddy Dunican** and **Paul Kennedy**, for holding me accountable and making sure I started writing this book.

To **Frazer Brookes**, for taking the courage and following your dream. You are a perfect role model of one doing what their heart desires. Thank you for your knowledge and training on social media, and for giving me a refreshing perspective on Facebook.

I am immensely thankful to have worked with the following great people on the Google Maps project, in Dublin. The **French Team**, **Marlis**, **Jagannath**, **Aleksander**, **Karolina**, **Radoslaw**, **Daniel P**, **Edyta Plawiak**, **Justyna T**, **Braien**, **Glenn**, **Ahmet**, **Mladen**, **Rubin**, **Mehmet**, **Murat**, **Melek**, **Claudiu**, **Jana**, **Sona**, **Hana**, **Blanca**, **Bruce**, **Michael M**, **Thomas S**, **Evelina**, **Shannon**, **Johnathan Hester**, **Matthias K**, **Jofferey V**, **Daphne**, **Saskia**, **Remy**, **Elias**, **Maartje**, **Eddy**, **Sarah D**, **Tom v/d Van**, **Kealan**, **Vivian**, **Flore**, **Julia A**, **Justine B**, **Renee Klumper**, **Ubaldo**, **Flavia**, **Sean Hynes**, **Viktor** and **Damaris**. The joy and laughter at the office and during lunch breaks is what lifted me up. It was through our friendships that I was inspired enough to write this book. You cheered and encouraged me from the beginning till the finishing of this book. **Eline**, **Torsten** and **Edyta Dolan**, thank you for giving me the Fridays off to write this book. **Mark Sutton**, thank you for your support and for helping me out with the title of this book.

Exchange Setbacks for Winning

To Free Chapel Senior Pastor, **Jentzen Franklin**, for your teachings on fasting; to me, you are the best person who explains this subject so well. It has impacted my life; thank you for making it simple.

To Lakwood Senior Pastor, **Joel Osteen**, for your inspirational and encouraging messages that you present weekly. It fuels my hope, and I am always uplifted when I listen to you or watch you on television. I recall playing your podcast messages over and over during some of my setbacks, and it often gave me strength to hold on to my dreams.

To **Cyrus Gorjipour** and **Salim Sander**, founders of Goalcast, for inspiring and encouraging me to leave my own lasting legacy. I have not only been elevated by Goalcast, but it also has helped me to write some of the chapters in this book.

I would like to thank co-founders, **Hugh Evans**, **Simon Moss**, **Wei Soo**, **Ryan Gall** and **Riot House,** from Global Citizen, for all their remarkable work, and for changing the lives of individuals, and making a difference in this world.

Finally, my appreciation to **Dyann Olivieira**, **Christina Fife**, **Waqas Ahmed, Lisa Browning** and **Sarah Flanagan,** for your special contribution, and for making this book possible.

CHAPTER 1

What Have You Been Told?

Invest in You
Invest in Others
Share Your Investment

How Much Are You Worth?

If someone came up to you and asked you, "**How much are you worth?**" what would your answer be? Let me clarify the question for you, to help you answer. How much are you worth in this life? Your value and sense of worth—is this priceless? Would you say you are worth more than anyone could ever pay you? Or would you say you are worth infinity beyond infinity?

What would it mean for you if you had given one of these answers?

Are you able to say, with confidence, "I am a high value person, worth more than anything, and no one could ever afford me?"

I am almost certain that most of us have not been asked, "How much are you worth?" and have never thought about this question either. And why is that? Is it an important question, and does it even matter?

I would say, *yes*. Yes, it's extremely important, as it can set the course of your life. Understanding this question can help you with your confidence, sense of worth, happiness, success, goals, and dreams in life. Let me tell you the story about the treasure.

Exchange Setbacks for Winning

When you were born, your parents did everything to protect you. You are their *treasure*; they kept you close, took care of you, and then they had to let you go. One day, the barriers around the treasure were taken off.

The treasure went out into the world—heard, touched, walked, felt, breathed—and was exposed to all kind of things he never had seen before.

The treasure heard words of discouragement: "Your grades are poor; nothing good will come from you."

The treasure touched the soccer ball, and was told, "You are stupid! You are supposed to kick the ball. Hahaha, and he thinks he is going to be a professional soccer player."

The treasure walked a long distance to catch the bus to his 8th job interview. After 3 days, he received the news that he was not successful.

The treasure's heart was broken when his first love told him, "I don't want to be with you anymore; I am in love with someone else."

The treasure could not breathe once he heard the news about the loss of one of his family members.

The treasure sees an article in the newspaper and in a magazine, stating gossip about him.

I am curious to know what you thought about the setbacks in the treasure's life.

Now, you might not have experienced the exact setbacks as the treasure, but to some degree, you can relate to some of the occurrences in his life. I know that I can. It seems that the treasure's self-esteem was constantly being tested and, if not managed well, he could lose his sense of worth and value. How I portray the treasure is what happens to most of us. Once we are old enough to stand on our own, we go out into the world to explore. You are not warned to guard your value with everything you have. Or to protect it and not allow anyone to change how you think about yourself. When we are ready to go out into the world, we hope to find ourselves and to achieve our deepest desires. Unfortunately, that's not what happens to the majority of us.

What Have You Been Told?

Setbacks—a familiar term—but you don't really know how it is until you experience it yourself. Setbacks: they can work in your favor when you're able to turn the situation around. The majority of us allow setbacks to take over our lives, and when that happens, we can lose our sense of direction in life. None of us is exempt from setbacks, but it can make your journey lighter when you understand what is going on. With over fifteen years of experience working with various clients, I bring you insight and awareness on this subject.

Family, friends, media, and society, as well as the environment we live in, have taught us to take most things at an average level. Unconsciously, they have passed on their mediocre attitude from their generation all the way up to today. This gives us the feeling of, and teaches some of us the following precepts:

You can have this but not that; you can only go so far; you are just…… so accept it; what makes you think you are better than….; you are not good enough; this is not for you, so perhaps let it go; if it is not working, it's just not working, so give up; you can't do that; you can't accomplish that.

You cannot ask THAT, and if you respond, asking WHY, they will reply, "That's BECAUSE," or you just CAN'T."….

The interesting thing is that they don't have the answers themselves as to why they are telling you why you cannot have or get something you would like to have.

Now imagine growing up all your life with all these limitations on yourself, and more damaging is that these are not only thoughts but they have become part of your belief system. If you grew up like that, then I want to tell you that it is not your fault! You cannot blame yourself, looking at yourself as an average person. You might have grown up in a very vibrant and positive environment, where your parents had invested in your sense of worth. You have a high opinion about your value, yet you are still not quite sure where life is taking you.

Perhaps you are that person with that feeling that won't go away.
"You know that feeling?"
"What feeling?"

That feeling that you are meant to be doing something different or greater—anything else but what you are currently doing—but you don't know what it is and how to do it. You believe there is more than just money. What is it that you can't put your finger on, which keeps you unsettled and frustrated at times? That feeling is very normal, and many people are experiencing the same. I had the same feeling at one point in my life, until I found my purpose in life. Your purpose is your success. Let me be more precise. Once you know who you are, and what you are meant to be doing, you become unstoppable; and once you are unstoppable, your success is inevitable.

My passion is for you to find your success on your own terms. I love seeing others succeed in life. I had the urge to share the words on these pages with you so you can go after your heart's desires. We are all meant to learn from one and other, and help others become the best version of themselves. I share my story— snippets of events, from a few of my setbacks to my success today. All the stories you are about to read in this book are true. The names have not been changed, except Nathan, Caitlin, Patrick, Ethan, and Mrs. Withly, for privacy reasons. I have deep respect for all the people whom I have written about in this book. I am also going to share stories of fascinating yet successful people to inspire you even more. My intention is for you to live up to your full potential and start ruling the world.

But before we move on, I need to share the following with you.

Since it is impossible to change anything without the permission and the decision of your mind, I choose not to give you an in-depth, step-by-step guide, or details, recommending exactly how to do things. I only share what you need to know to succeed in life. I knew I had to start with your mind first, to help you discover your vision and how to take the first step. I know that if I can change your mind, you could believe and alter anything in your life. I have full confidence in you, and believe you would know what to do once you understand and shift a few mindsets I share in this book.

If I can do what I love, you can do the same. My first goal is to help you stand above your setbacks, and provide you with the insight that

What Have You Been Told?

setbacks are the major distracters of where you want to be in life—your destiny.

Second, I wish to inspire and assist you in creating the life you truly want.
- What you always wanted to do in your career
- To live a happier life
- To be fulfilled and content in life
- To have a reason to get up each morning
- To be successful in all the areas of your life

By the end of this book you will...
Invest in You
- Understand the power of your mind
- Know what you're meant to be doing—your life purpose.
- Know how to build your confidence and reconnect with your *why*
- Have an unshakable belief in yourself and your dreams
- Enjoy your life more

Invest in Others
- Identify your gifts and talents and use it to your advantage— your signature, your way of giving back to the world.

Share Your Investment
- Know how to grow the career you truly want
- Understand the importance of creating financial success

I have included writing space at the end of each chapter for you to write down all your thoughts and ideas. I have named these pages the *Investment Page*. I have also designed an *Inspirational Notebook*, for you called *Follow Your Dreams,* where you can journal all your thoughts, ideas and vision. You can get your copy at www.ExchangeAndWinLife.com.

I hope you have not given up on your dreams but are ready to start a new chapter in your life. Take on this exciting adventure and change your life forever. Yes, forever! Exchange your setbacks for winning today, and unlock the secrets to a prosperous life.

If you read this book till the end, and apply the life changing principles, you guarantee yourself an extraordinary personal and professional life.

I wish you a successful and fantastic journey as you create an incredible life for yourself.

Your greatest life is in front of you.

Change for the Better

I always knew I wanted to publish books; I just didn't know when—until one day after I finished up with a client.

The last client just walked out the door. With a deep sigh, I thought to myself, I have seen many families' lives transformed. Children who couldn't walk or speak, I helped them to walk and speak, and they became part of my life. I have fought for the rights of several children. One, in particular, I will never forget: five-year-old Patrick and I had worked hard on some of his impairments. Exceptionally, he had improved on his ability, over nine months, from severe to mild autism. His parents, family, and I were all so happy to see the growth and changes in his life. When the time came and the parents had to choose a school for Patrick, we all wanted to make sure his hard work wasn't wasted. I put my hand up, undertaking an assessment with The Department of Education to prove and demonstrate the improvement of Patrick's ability—his independence. Long story short, Patrick got accepted at the school his parents hoped for him to go.

I have walked the journey with a suicidal client whom, today, is enjoying life and not looking for a way to escape anymore. The client who came in depressed is now able to manage and control her mind. She has learned to turn her focus from herself, and she has found

What Have You Been Told?

strength from within. With my help, she is able to recognize negative emotions that most of us all go through. Individuals from all walks of life have found hope and strength again after they came to see me. As a professional counsellor and behavioral therapist, I have expressed and stressed the importance of one finding their purpose in life.

Standing in my office, I was thinking about all the various lives I had been involved with, and all the clients whom I had impacted. They had helped me see and appreciate the simplest things in life. They helped me as much as I helped them. I always enjoyed hearing, seeing, and witnessing the positive changes in my clients' lives, and that was always my reward. It was my drug, my XTC, my drive and excitement—that's what got me up in the morning.

"This is not enough; this is not enough," I kept saying out loud.

"No!" There must be more to this, I am not helping enough; I am not reaching enough people. Surely, this can't be it. I loved being in my private practice; yet I felt that staying in this field was not where the *helping people story* ends.

While walking to the kitchen to get a glass of water, I recalled what my grandmother, Dorthy, had said: "Cynthia, you are born to help others. The world is not for you alone; you're meant to share who you are with others. No matter how people treat you, good or bad, you need to serve others. I know with all my heart that you are going to be great by serving people." I was five when my grandmother said those beautiful and encouraging words to me. While still in the kitchen, I then knew the exact year I wanted to publish my book, and I aimed for 2016.

There is enough for each and all of us to do. While we live here on earth, we are all meant to find out what we are supposed to do. If people truly can become whatever they can become, there would be less suffering on the earth. Based on the many clients I have helped over the years, when asked about their purpose in life, the average person doesn't know what they want to do. When asked, "What would you really like to do?" most responses are, "I don't know." I never believed that for a second.

Exchange Setbacks for Winning

Often people say, "I don't know," because, first, they haven't taken the time to think about what they would like to do. They say, "I don't know," to escape or avoid the question. Secondly, the major cause of the answer, "I don't know," is the suppression of life difficulties that one faced, and I am not excluded from it. I know what it is like to be pressured by setback, so here is my story.

Born in Ghana, in a small town called Suhum, my biological parents, Peter and Comfort, left me behind with Grandmother Dorthy and Aunty Rebecca, whom I call *Mother*. Growing up, for as long as I can remember, I've called Rebecca my mother, and together we have bonded a strong mother and daughter relationship. Comfort's existence was unknown to me until I moved to the Netherlands, at age 5. I was shocked to find out, and at an early age, I became slightly depressed about the news. I was told to love Comfort more than Rebecca; I tried and failed. Until present, that strong bond has not been broken; if anything, it has grown stronger. Not to confuse you, but today, if you hear me say *Mother*, I am referring to Rebecca.

At age 4, Rebecca left Ghana to live in the Netherlands, and shortly after that, at age 5, I reunited with her in Amsterdam. I can't describe to you how happy I was to see my mother again. Between the ages of five and fifteen, I used to spend hours in the library, reading as many books as possible. I love books and visiting libraries; being surrounded by thousands and thousands of books was, and still is, my favorite thing to do.

At 6, one afternoon after school, I found my mother, Comfort, anxious and upset. She said, "Cynthia, your dad has not been home since yesterday. We need to go to the police station and report him missing." We didn't know where he was until 1 week later: Peter came home, and from that day on, everything changed at home. The arguments between Peter and Comfort were increasing, and the fights were frequently about finances and Peter's absence.

I started writing at 8. I would often write in my journals, and wrote letters to my friends. Sometimes to express how I was feeling, and other times, it was also my escape from the world I was living in. I felt very sorry for Comfort; I saw how dependent she was, and vulnerable, and thought she was very unlucky. I then made a promise to myself not to walk the same journey as her. At age 10, Grandmother passed away, and I did not take that well. I cried myself to sleep for the next 7 years. I often had nightmares, especially on bad days at home; so much so that I had suicidal thoughts. I wanted to die to be with grandmother, because I always felt safe around her. After age fifteen, I read less and less: the only books I read at that time were educational books. I had to read them for college or university, and today, when I look back, I really regret not keeping the pace up for reading different books. I never lost my passion for books, but reading many books became a chore.

Things started to get really bad at home, as my biological parents were arguing more and more; the physical and mental abuse was not getting less but more scary.

At age 16, I ran away from home, as it was no longer safe for me to live in the same house with Peter. I could not take the abuse anymore and had to protect myself from him. From age 17, I often had two jobs; I worked hard to pay for my education, and I was determined to live differently than Comfort had. Meanwhile, I won the court case against my parents, and it was now officially declared unsafe to live with them. My parents got a warning that if one of their children came forward again, all their children would be taken away from them and handed over to social services. I was disowned and abandoned by the entire family, from the age of 18. The last time I saw Peter and Comfort, and my 3 biological sisters, was when I was 19 years old. There was no communication after that.

At 23, I moved to Australia to study, and I graduated with a Bachelor of Theology and a postgraduate degree in counseling. While growing up, it was not even on my agenda to pursue any degrees, because Peter had often said, "Cynthia, you are stupid." Sadly enough, I believed him, but only until the age of 19. Surprisingly, although living in an abusive home, I was doing well at school and had excellent grades. I made a pact with myself at age 10—to make sure I would not end up dependent on anyone, I believed education was my way out, and it came to fulfillment.

Between the ages of 25 and 32, I worked in the retail sector. I also worked for 2 1/2 years as a school counsellor, and a couple of years in the corporate world, but all this was never fulfilling. I still had the desire to have something for myself, and I wanted to be my own boss. I then started to think in that direction but soon established that I did not know where to start. This statement highlights the third reason why people would answer, "I don't know," to their life purpose. Like myself, none of us have been taught, other than to study successful people, *how to pursue your dreams*. You are about to read how I woke myself up, a couple of years ago, to this dilemma. Here are my findings:

I wish school had taught me...

Why was I not told or taught how to do it?

To do what?

To become the best me, to use all my talents and gifts, to strive, to manage my life successfully, to empty out the potential that is inside me.

I had heard that I could become anything I wanted to be, but how do you become what you aspire to be?

What resources do I need, and where do I go from here to look for the best and the right resources. Who do I talk to, and where can I find someone who could teach me how they became successful.

While thinking about all these questions, I could see countless pictures in my head: I imagined; I visualized; I saw visions, and my dreams were endless. All these numerous idea's—I didn't know where to start. I looked around, and it was easy to become complacent; it didn't take much effort. Deep inside, dreams and thoughts of new ideas and different creativities rushed through my head. Man! This can't be right!

I snapped back and asked myself another question, "How come there are some people out there who are doing what they love doing, and I am not?" I see them using their gifts and talents, and the best part is, they also get paid tons of money for what they love doing, and they are financially free. In contrast, today, many researchers believe that the average individual is not happy with their career or life in

What Have You Been Told?

general, and I could not agree more. It is a known fact that 85% of people today hate their jobs. I am happier when I am writing or sharing my knowledge, and impacting the lives of others through the act of service and kindness. That's what makes me really happy!

Whilst most people dislike their job and secretly are looking for a way out, others have settled for convenience and have chosen to take life as it comes. When you stop trying, or start thinking negatively about your plans, that's when you unconsciously put your plans on hold. Putting your plans on hold means a delay, and a delay means it's going to take a little longer, right? Crazy enough, for some people, they put their plans on hold for the rest of their lives. The danger in not completing your initial desired plan is that you end up with something called *second best*.

I don't believe people absolutely want to live an ordinary life. I refuse to believe that we were born to work with no purpose or meaning, just paying bills and accepting the unhappy stage as final. I trust that people have strong desires to live a significant life, but the problem is that they don't know how to. Unfortunately, our schools don't stress or emphasize enough to go after what we truly want in life, but teach you and me to get any job that comes along. It's as if they are almost saying, "Make sure you find a job; you don't need to love it—just make sure you find one to cover your expenses." Idealistically, entrepreneurship should be included in our education system, and the opportunity should be presented for one to choose, teaching innovation, how to create jobs, and to avoid the modern rat race.

I was shocked to see how many people had fallen for the lie: the lie of *"there couldn't be more than this."* The majority of people believe the common phrase, "This is it," doing what everyone else is doing. Today, that statement makes sense to me because that's what people know to do and, therefore, they can't tell you to do something different from what they are already doing. None of us have been given the tools or strategies to become who we really want to become. Having gone through the Dutch and Australian education system, I can't say I was taught. Plus, I have never heard anyone communicate that they had been shown how to become successful at school. If you have been, please let me know, because that means you went to an awesome school.

At age 32, I started my private practice, and at age 33, with a lot of struggle, I received my permanent residence in Australia. Maybe, one day, I will tell the full story, but not today. Meanwhile, I was extremely happy. Finally, no more setbacks, I thought; I can now enjoy what's ahead of me. Things were looking good for the first time. I was doing great in my career and called myself blessed. I was thankful for my amazing friends and family, and I felt good spiritually and mentally. I was driven by my goals and could not wait to see more of my dreams unfolding. I decided to get back into writing, and I aimed to publish my first book.

Setbacks: we all go through them, but how we rise above them is what matters.

Investment Page

- How do you perceive yourself?
- What do you believe about yourself?
- Do you believe more what your friends, family, and other people say about you?
- Are you a strong minded person and modest about your value?
- Do you believe me when I say, "You are worth more than anything?"
- Is this all foreign to you because that's not the way you grew up?

Write your answers on the Investment Page

I had no idea that my life was about to take a 180 degree turn. To find out how, keep reading. I will also show you how setbacks can work in your favor.

What Have You Been Told?

Investment Page

CHAPTER 2

Setbacks

When You Least Expect

Sydney, May 2015. One week after my birthday, I decided to pay a visit to the doctor, and I undertook a health test. Early the next day, I received the phone call: "Cynthia, you are low in iron, and you will have to go to the emergency room for iron infusion. You should not be walking around; it's a miracle really that you are walking around. This is protocol, Cynthia; it is not safe for you to be at work or anywhere else but the hospital," Dr. Roberts said. "Emergency! Hospital! What do you mean?" I thought. That doesn't sound good. Suddenly, I felt my life being reversed. "What is this?" One moment you can be on the direct path, and then you experience another setback. "When is this going to end?" I screamed inside. Just when I thought I was getting back on track, once again there is another disruption.

Packing my bag, I had to make sure to bring the referral letter from Dr. Roberts. I grabbed my car keys and jumped in the car, thinking I should be back in a couple of hours. Once at the hospital, I gave the referral letter to the lady behind the counter. "Ms. Asante, just wait here; I will call a nurse to attend to you." Hmmm, strange that she did not say that I could take a seat. I know that this hospital is known for slow services. "Ms. Asante, please come with me, and please take a seat," the nurse said. "I am looking at your numbers, and it is a miracle that you are walking around; you could have dropped dead. How did you get here?" "I drove," I said.

"Well, you will have to call someone to pick you up, as you will not be able to drive home." "Really," I said surprisingly.

"I don't think you understand how low your iron level is, Ms. Asante. It is lower than a pregnant woman's, and if we were to measure you in batteries, you would only have 20% left of iron in your body." I had no understanding of my condition until the nurse broke it down for me.

For the next two weeks, I was bedridden. My body was poisoned, and I was feeling more ill than before. For the next three months, I was receiving an iron infusion twice a week, as my body was still low in iron. I felt like a heroin addict. In the meantime, I was scheduled to have surgery. The doctors advised the removal of cervical polyps. Hopefully, this would stop the heavy and serious bleeding, not to mention the cramps and hormonal confusion in my body. The surgery was successful, but that did not solve the problem. I was still bleeding heavily and had to have more tests.

January 2016. Sitting in the gynecologist's waiting room, I was not sure what to think or to feel. This is the day when I would hear what the next step forward would be. "Cynthia, we have looked at your case and have discussed this with other doctors, and there is nothing we can do at the moment. We can't perform another surgery, as it would mean that you would lose your womb and be hemorrhaging, and at the moment, it is too risky. You are young, but it is not safe for us to do the surgery; it is life threatening."

I had been diagnosed with a life threatening illness—a tumor called a fibroid—which was growing, sucking, collecting, and storing blood for itself on top of my womb. It seemed that I had no chance of beating this giant inside me. The 30-minute drive home was devastating and painful; I felt pain all over my body. I cried all the way from the hospital to home. My tears were unstoppable and, by the time I reached home, I was exhausted from this shocking news. I ran to my bedroom, grabbed a cushion, hid my face in it, and screamed so loud—I didn't care if the neighbors heard me or not. How could this be? My head was spinning. Am I going to walk on this earth for the rest of my life without a womb? And that would also mean no children. How can this be taken away from me? Not that I wished that upon anyone, but I didn't understand this, and questioned, "Why me?" For the next 2 weeks, I would go to bed crying, and with tears in my eyes, I would wake up. I still remember the 2 weeks as if it was yesterday. As soon as I woke up, the tears were the first thing that greeted me. I was crying 24/7—if you did not see my tears, I was crying inside.

February 2016. I received a phone call from Akua, a mother figure and a good friend.

She wanted me to meet Dr. Hanafy, who is one of the co-founders of the uterus transplantation concept. He had performed the world's first uterus transplant, in Sweden, in 2012. Akua was convinced that he could help with my critical case. I took her advice, as Sydney doctors had closed the door on me.

Sitting with Dr. Hanafy, and after explaining my case, he said the following: "I can understand why the Sydney doctors didn't want to undergo the surgery. You've got a complicated case, and it is risky for sure, but it is not impossible." With confidence, he continued, "I can do the surgery for you; I will take up the challenge because I know it is possible."

My hope ignited when I heard those words: *it is possible*. I felt that I had received my miracle already. "The only thing is that you will lose the top part of your womb, but the rest should be fine. The fibroid sits right on top of your womb, and in order to remove it, we will have to cut some of your womb. That's your problem, Cynthia. Where the fibroid is position that would cause you to hemorrhage. With all that being said, the decision is yours," Dr. Hanafy said. Not able to think straight, I asked the following: "What would happen if I don't do the surgery?"

"The fibroids will grow larger, and will eventually, slowly, affect your other organs." This sounded right, as I had already experienced unusual tiredness and painful symptoms. By this stage, I looked 5 months pregnant, and I experienced a mixture of menopause symptoms and heavy menstruation that would go on for weeks at a time, along with a pregnant woman's hormones, all at once.

The Phone Call

Queensland, May 2016. I woke up with an oxygen mask on my face. The cannula in my right arm had fluids running, and the cannula in my left arm had blood transfusing. The next thing I felt was the catheter, "What is that?" I thought. I lifted up the blanket and saw a tube collecting my urine. I struggled to move my legs; the compression stockings were sticking out of the calf compressor. I guessed this was to massage my legs to help circulate the blood. I was freezing and had this unbearable pain that I can't describe to you. The nurse walked in and explained that I was connected to a pump that gave me the ability to provide myself with pain relief when I needed it. All I had to do was push the red button, and it would administer morphine through the cannula.

That same day, in the afternoon, Dr. Hanafy came to check on me; things were looking good, and he announced the surgery to be successful. With a joyful heart, I was pleased to hear that the large, orange-size fibroid had been removed, and I still had my womb.

Around 8pm, I started experiencing heavy bleeding. I had been on the blood transfusion all day but still needed another pack to be delivered. I already lost a tremendous amount of blood during the surgery, so I needed every drop. I couldn't afford to lose more blood at this stage. Then, what we were all afraid of, happened. Within less than 2 hours, I was lying in a pool of blood.

Lying on the hospital bed, I had no doubt, and believed, that God had promised to preserve my womb and my life, and I did not see this coming. I was losing more blood. I recalled the meeting with Dr. Hanafy: "The chance for you to hemorrhage is almost inevitable, and that's why the Sydney doctors wouldn't touch you. But I believe it is possible to do this surgery, and I will do anything to save your womb. I will do everything in my power, with my team, to save it, Cynthia; because I know how important this is for a woman like yourself."

Within the next hour, I had been changed 3 times, there had been a flood of blood coming from inside me, and I was literally lying in a pool of blood. Even the nurse, who had been working for the last 17 years, had never seen so much blood before. I felt pain all over my body; I was cold, and saw the nurse through a blurry effect. I was struggling to breathe and was thankful for the oxygen mask that helped me breathe. In my head, I was telling myself to stay conscious and to hold on. "You must stay awake, Cynthia." I started to feel weaker and weaker. The nauseous feeling was getting worse and, as I felt the vomit coming up, I quickly turned myself to lie on my side. I remember this from working with clients and from the first aid course; and today, it came in handy. The nurse quickly grabbed a towel and placed another one underneath my head for support. After things settled a bit, I heard her saying, "I am going to call the doctor."

I managed to reach my phone on the side table, and I made my 3 top phone calls, just in case they were to lose me. I called Rebecca first and said, "Mom, it seems that it has come to that point; I am not doing well, and I need you to pray." I didn't want to scare her too much and did not share any excessive information. I was pleased to hear her voice; her voice always gives me strength. "Sevda, the bleeding is not stopping; please pray that I will make it through the night." "Akua, please pray, as I am feeling very sick." The life machine beeped repeatedly. At a distance, I could see the nurse reaching out for the red button on the wall to buzz the emergency team. My heart beat was dropping, and I went unconscious. I don't know for how long. I opened my eyes and saw a total of 6 people in my room: 1 consultant nurse; the assistant nurse, who had been taking care of me; and 4 members of the emergency team. The emergency team had been buzzed in twice already, and this was the second time they had to come in. Dr. Hanafy was still not there.

Will I Make It Through the Night?

I can't exactly remember what time Dr. Hanafy walked in, but I remember how he walked in. From the door to my bed, he took his time, and with a calm and confident manner, he finally reached my bed. In that moment, it seemed as if he would never arrive. He asked everyone to leave the room, except the nurse who had been by my side since this nightmare started. With Dr. Hanafy in the room, I felt relieved and hopeful, and I trusted him to have a solution. Before the surgery, I had been praying for God to give him the wisdom to save my womb, and my life. While he was standing next to my bed, I could see him thinking. With his arms half crossed, he rubbed his index finger over his chin, and said the following: "I know of this medication that will help reduce the bleeding. This should buy us time; we are looking at a minimum of 6 hours to 8 hours maximum. Hopefully, I will have figured out what we can do; and, as promised, I will do anything to protect your womb. I will go and get the suppository myself, and bring it to the nurse to administer to you. I also will have to call Akua. I know we don't want to scare her, but it is my duty to give her a call and inform her of the critical state you are in."

It was 1:30 a.m. Akua received the phone call, since she was the person to contact for any emergencies. She also had taken on the responsibility of taking care of me after the surgery—although we all trusted God that he would get me through the surgery and keep me alive. At the end of the day, it was all up to God if I would live again, with either 3/4 of my womb, no womb but alive, or no life at all. It was all up to the Almighty God, and if the unexpected would have happened, Akua would have been the one to deliver the bad news to Rebecca and to the rest. I don't exactly know what Dr. Hanafy said during the phone conversation with Akua, but the main message was, "Cynthia is not doing well; the situation is critical, and she has been bleeding non-stop. We are watching her closely, and I have assigned a nurse to watch her; she is with her in the room." The minute Akua hung up the phone, she went next door to her daughter's room. "Amma, wake up; we have to pray for Cynthia." Till today, I am very thankful for Rebecca, Sevda, and Akua's prayers throughout the night. Looking back today, it is very comforting to know that between midnight until the morning, I had people pleading for my life, and for the next generation that would come from me.

Setbacks

Is There a Way Out?

After battling through the night, dawn came, and I probably had 2 hours of sleep. It was a miracle! The suppository saved my life—the bleeding had completely stopped. In the history of Dr. Hanafy's work, no other doctor, or himself, had ever administered the type of suppository to a patient who just had undergone a major surgery. Till today, I am so blessed that he thought of that medication. I can't imagine what would have happened.

While the nurse was changing the empty pack of blood, I felt exhausted; it was as if I had climbed Mount Everest. For the next 24 hours, I was going to be on the blood transfusion, topping up all that had been lost. After a week, I wanted to recover at home, plus I was paying a $1000 a night out of my pocket. With two amazing friends, with a profession in the medical field, I knew I was in good hands, and was discharged.

Unexpectedly, I slipped into depression during my recovery at home. I felt lost and could not see any good thing happening for my future. I started to question the purpose of my existence. I looked back and everything seemed pointless, as I believed I had lost everything I had worked for. I had to start over again, and I didn't know how. I questioned myself again, "Is there a way out?" Then I remembered what the doctors, nurses, and the anesthetist had said, "It is normal for you to feel extreme pain after your surgery, and you can overcome the suffering." Though I felt defeated, I knew that it wasn't the truth, and I decided to work hard to overcome the dependency and vulnerability phase. A month later, I had reduced the doses I was taking, and I started to feel better. I believed the medications, especially the Endone tablets, were causing the depression too.

Finally, I had my wake-up call. "Cynthia, *you have been given a second chance to live, and what are you going to do about it?*"

While searching within myself, I looked setbacks in the eye and discovered that **setbacks are only distracters or detours of our dreams**. I realized that the challenges in the process of going through disappointments is what causes distractions. During the process, we might feel stress, overwhelmed, or have no sense of direction for a cause. The average person gives up along the way when faced with difficult times, instead of taking the responsibility to continue pursuing their dreams.

Nothing is final, and setbacks have an end. Life challenges are temporary, like the seasons of life. Everything is subject to change, so don't allow discouragement to overwhelm you. Lift your head up, and believe that great things are yet to come. While you keep taking steps forward, and don't lose heart, whatever you're believing or hoping for, eventually you will get your breakthrough. Your impetus, actions, and faith are the forces behind your goals and dreams. The moment you start putting actions behind your goals and dreams, you shift things into gear. Uncomfortable situations will come, and you will make mistakes, but with time, you will learn to manage your setbacks. Keep going, and you will learn to look back for knowledge, and look forward to make a difference in your own life and that of others. If you have not seen the result yet, it means whatever you are looking for is still in progress; therefore, it is not finished yet. It's on its way and still coming.

Meanwhile, in that moment, I knew what I wanted: to live a large and more fulfilling life. I wanted change. I didn't want to live the life I had been living, and I believe there is always more: to see my childhood dream perfected, have a bigger impact, and see people's lives change for the better. I share my story with you to offer evidence of the possibilities in life, and that you can truly live the life you want. I believe nothing is impossible. Look around you. Others have done it; that's proof enough for you and me.

We are all works in progress.

* To see a full-sized, colored picture of the doctors who saved my life, and to see me in the hospital, go to www.ExchangeAndWinLife.com.

Setbacks

You Can't Quit!

I don't know what you have gone through so far, or what your setbacks are; whatever it is, I want to say the following to you:

Like myself, every step you have taken so far has brought you to where you are today. You might not feel strong within, and can feel lost or confused at times. Know that you are stronger than you think. You have come so far, and you are still here and alive. Most importantly, I love how you choose to better yourself. It tells me that you are full of hope. *Hope is the engine of your life. Without hope, you can't go anywhere.* As you keep stretching forward, you are getting a day closer to where you want to be. You are getting closer and closer, so keep going and don't stop. If you need to rest along the way, rest, pause, or slow down, and take the pace up again when you are ready. But whatever you do, DO NOT QUIT; quitting is not an option and should never be on your list. You do not gain anything from surrendering; it only prevents you from seeing what you could have become or achieved. There is an inner power within you, and it is there for you to tap into. It is always there, waiting for you to take the steps together. Let resilience be your friend— you have the ability to get back on your feet whenever you want. The key here is to make sure you get up, keep moving, keep your head up, and don't let your eyes look away from hope.

In the midst of toughness, it's not how you fall but how you get up and get back into shape. Once again, I want you to get this: YOU are stronger than you think. You have come so far, so why not push a little bit further and further and further. All successful people have one thing in common: they never give up on themselves. They do not stop or quit but walk the walk until they are living in their dream, instead of looking at the dream. With that in mind, you can also live in your dream and make it a reality. Dreams: believe you can, and you're halfway there.

You can slow down but don't give up.

Setbacks in Your Favor

I have watched many clients experience setbacks, and I have seen how they managed to exchange their setbacks for winning. They took on a new way of looking at their circumstances, and they learned to use their complicated times to their advantage. If there's anyone I know and respect, who has also exchanged their setbacks for winning, it is Steve Jobs. The following is an example of an interesting, uplifting story.

Imagine that you are unemployed and are looking for employment.

You can say to me, "Cynthia, I have tried everything; I still haven't found a job." Generally speaking, most people will lose a job at least once in their life, or they might be going through it now. Steve Jobs did not let the stigma of unemployment limit his success in life. Jobs was forced to resign from his own company, in 1985. He looked for a new pathway after his dismissal, and continued working on his passion, in his garage. I guess none of us knew that he was working on the iPod. While he had not given up on himself and pursuing his passion, he became more creative. In his persistence, he found ways and opportunities that served him in the end. During that time, Jobs became the founder of Pixar and NeXT. In 1997, Steve Jobs became CEO of his former company, and in 2001, he introduced the first iPod. In 2007, he launched the first iPhone; and today, we are all familiar with the iPhone and all the other Apple products.

I hope I have gotten the point across. Who knows, if Jobs had not been forced out of Apple, Pixar and NeXT might not have been developed. The difficult period became an advantage for Jobs, as it served him to discover his true potential. With that in mind, applying for new employment is great, but let that not be your main focus—work on your other talents. This could be anything from volunteering to pursuing some of your greatest desires. You must continuously develop what you most love doing, and see where it can take you. Keep chasing your passion, and this will get you to where you want to be in life.

Setbacks

Setbacks are only detours, if we keep going. A detour is not a destination but a delay. You can delay your dream, but don't allow your setback to become your destination.

> **Investment Page**
>
> Here are 4 insightful questions that clients have found useful. This is to support you in approaching your setbacks differently from what you might have been doing.
>
> - Can you see anything positive in your situation (what you're facing)?
> - How can you use the challenge to your advantage?
> - Look at your strengths. Can you name them?
> - Do you believe your situation can work for you and be an advantage to you?
>
> Write your answers on the Investment Page.

Setbacks can make it hard for you think clearly. Emotionally, you can feel stuck at times. But don't worry; I will show you, in the next chapter, how to recognize your emotional patterns, the ones that cause mental blocks and stop you from thinking straight and identifying what you normally enjoy doing, as well as how to discipline your mind in every season of life.

Investment Page

CHAPTER 3

Be Aware

Strength

One day, I was talking to a young man who I had met at the airport, and while we were waiting to board the plane, he shared his story with me. Ethan made the statement, "Life can be just so hard at times." "Tell me more," I said. "Well," Ethan said, as he paused and took a deep breath, "I have been feeling alone, and nobody knows about it. I have days where I feel that nobody understands me. I have tried things, but nothing seems to be working for me. There are some days where I want to cave in or escape, but then I don't even know where to go. For the last couple years, I have felt pain—pain over and over again—not to mention the confusion, frustration, and sadness that comes with it. Days like this, I wonder if I am the only one who has these thoughts and feelings. People around me—my friends, family, and colleagues—in my eyes, they seem to have it all together." Ethan paused again, looked away, and took another deep breath. He continued saying, "I then have another close look at my life. My mind takes me back and forth, between the past and the future, where it seems as if all my dreams are locked away. In the midst of this interchange, for a couple of seconds, I see a glimpse of my dreams, and this gives me a great sense of joy, happiness, and contentment. But then, my mind takes me back to the present moment, the reality. I have asked myself many, many times, "How can I change this situation? How I am feeling?"

I don't know about you, but there have been times where I have felt like Ethan.

Exchange Setbacks for Winning

When life hits you at your worst, you tend to forget to look at what you have. Even more serious, you can't even see what you've got; and therefore, you fail to be thankful for what you do have. Intense hardship can take you so deep that your surroundings can fade away in the front of your eyes. You stop enjoying the activities you used to do, socializing becomes less attractive, and you would rather be left alone or hide. Your mood swings increase, and your loved ones can become victims of your frustration. To make matters worse, you don't even have an explanation for your own behavior. You get caught up in your own world and, if you are not careful, life passes you by. Is it me, or have you also noticed that in our time, the average person lives a rushed lifestyle. People want things to be done quickly, and patience is more of a bothering factor than a virtue. We have allowed the pressure of the world to take us away from *living in the moment*. Once, a client of mine asked me what it means to be in the *present moment*. In short, I said, "It is t*o become aware of your surroundings, to exist, and to take control of the state of mind during the moment you're in.* I will give you a glimpse of how it looks when you don't *live in the present moment.*

If I may use you as an example, let's say you are having a conversation with somebody, or you are spending time with your children. During that stage, your physical body is present, but your mind, thoughts, and feelings are absent and not engaged with the phase of living. At that exact point of time, you have not given yourself fully to the situation. But then, of course, this is not done on purpose. The only thing is that neither you nor the people you are spending time with are being acknowledged or enjoyed to the fullest. This oblivious behavior is very common, and is in each and every one of us; nevertheless, we can learn to manage.

To live in the moment, and to recognize the state of mind you're in, you will need to create a clear headspace. Choose to be present with your whole body, especially your mind. Eliminate thoughts that are not relevant to the present moment, and only focus on what is necessary. Clarity helps you to navigate and to take steps forward. In other words, a sound mind decision is often birth from a free spirit.

Be Aware

You are guaranteed to make the best and the most of your situation, from the right state of mind. Towards the end of this chapter, I share some precise ideas on how to master your mind.

I would like to tell you that you will not go through any disappointments from now on, but then I would be lying to you. Disappointments come and go throughout our life time, and some of them are beyond our control. And you can feel unsubstantial when it comes your way, and there is nothing wrong with that. Our weakness is often also our strength; it teaches us life lessons and, during our time of need, we adopt new life skills. Some challenges are short, and we are able to find solutions for them, and others are long term. Sometimes they can drag on for weeks, months, or years, and discourage us. And if we don't pay close attention, they can take over our lives. Consequently, we can blame and feel guilty about the situation. There is not much you can do about the past, as that's gone, but you can always do something about the future. Don't miss out on the most important things in your life; stay in the moment, with the goal of bringing the future to the present.

There is always strength left in you.

Watch Out for Your Emotions

Although setbacks are seen as an external source, unfortunately, the issue lies deeper than that. During setbacks, your emotions are tested like never before. It can take you either way, to a positive or negative direction.

Think back to a time in your life when you were in love, and how you felt. That epic, exciting, happy feeling had your adrenaline so high you probably thought you owned the world. I remember when I first fell in love: I felt very happy and excited, and I had butterflies in my stomach every time I thought of the person. Walking on the main street of the shops, with a big smile on my face, people walking past me, it felt as if I was the only one on that street. In my own world, the rough push from the man with the grey winter coat meant nothing to me. He apologized, saying, "Sorry, sorry, sorry." "It's okay," I responded. Though I felt a light pain in my shoulder, I really didn't care. I guess I was not paying attention and did not watch where I was walking.

Another time, I received excellent news, and this news was very important to me as I had been waiting for it for over a year at that time. The phone call confirmed that I was granted a permanent visa for Australia. I can't explain to you the abundance of joy I was feeling. I recall jumping around, and I couldn't wait to share the good news with loved ones.

An interesting factor is that often when we find ourselves with feelings described as above, we feel like we are on top of the world. It does not matter what happened to us—that day, we feel like a winner. Somebody could come and yell at us, but we wouldn't care less. Suddenly, everything or any other problem seems like a small matter to us in that moment.

So, what was happening with my emotions and my mind? Unconsciously, my focus during that moment was on the (happy) event that caused that positive energy. You and I both know that positive occurrences do not make other life issues disappear.

As long as we have that positive feeling going, the chemicals are not only generated throughout our body but also to our mind. While the positive energy is still present, we feel in control, whether it is during a difficult season or not. Research has discovered that it is possible to be in a happy state of mind and yet experience a complicated situation.

Have you ever bought an item from a shop, and a day or week later, you saw it on sale for a very low price? I definitely have, on many occasions, and all I could think was, "I bought it for full price; I feel ripped off." I am sure you have had moments in your life where you have felt *short changed*. Now, this paragon is light and simple—nothing serious for you to let your emotions run wild about.

There are some individuals and families who go through more serious adversities, from mild to severe and traumatic events. It is unthinkable what a human can go through. The various turmoil that comes with all kinds of emotions during the setback period is unbelievable. At times, you might feel stressed, depressed, anxious, overwhelmed, confused, angry, or sad. Maybe life has not been easy on you, and you still have not figured matters out after all these years. Others seem to have it all together—well, that is what it looks like anyway. You might then think, "Life is not fair," and feel short changed. Yes, life might not seem fair, and we tend to blame others for our problems at times. Such statements stem from our thoughts and emotions, especially when we feel disappointed or confused.

Your emotions are connected to your experience in life, whether it is in the moment or the past. For instance, in both previous scenarios, the emotional state was triggered by the external. Something happened that caused me to feel good, happy, bad, or sad. Those feelings are chemical reactions.

Here are some great recommendations that clients have found practical:

- Change the situation, event, or environment you're in (e.g., Let's say you are at home; then perhaps go for a walk, drive, or visit a friend.).
- Write in your journal; express your thoughts and feelings on paper.
- Go over your dreams and imagine new visions.
- Listen to or watch motivational podcasts; go out and take some pictures in nature; draw or paint.
- Listen to some uplifting music (make sure you don't listen to music that's going to make you sad).
- Call a friend, coach, mentor, or family member, or anyone you can trust, or a helpline.
- Do an activity you used to enjoy.

Do whatever you feel comfortable with, but promise me that you will do something to turn your focus from you.

With this insight and understanding, hopefully I have increased your self-awareness regarding your emotions. Try and learn to manage your emotions and pay attention to how you think throughout the day. Be observant at all times, as you can't afford to stray from your purpose in life.

To take control of your emotions is to be in charge of your mind.

The Internal Confident

Have you noticed that you tend to reach out more to others and do more activities when you are in a better mood? For instance, calling a friend or family member to go out, cooking or purchasing a nice meal for yourself, or booking the holiday you have been putting off for a while. It is much easier to please ourselves and others when we are in the right state of mind. This is when you feel happy and at peace mentally. When things don't go as planned, especially when you feel stressed, it's harder to think or to be there for others. When that happens, some of us can feel lost, out of balance, or disconnected from the world. Your life can feel restricted. Know that no matter how you feel, you are still in charge of your life, though it might not feel like it. Make a decision and don't allow the outside world take over. Refuse to accept negative outsources, rather operate the issue from the inside.

What you truly need and want is to tap into your *internal confidant*. This is a personal acceptance and assurance of oneself, knowing when and what direction to spend your energy. We all have an internal confidant that we forget to access when we experience setbacks. It's very simple: you'll have to choose to step above what you see, and believe in what you don't see. What you don't see is what you hope to see manifested. The key is to keep your belief system and mind under discipline. Judge your energy, and spend it to believe in what you want, not to invest in what is holding you back.

When you feel in control of your life, it liberates you to act on the external. Your perception is much clearer and, as a result, you create more space to be friendly, or to be generous, to act kind, and to support others. Your experience at that stage comes from a state of happiness and gives you positive vibes. Internally, your sense of fulfillment and contentment is enhanced when your focus is on something else. You are then able to reach out for more—more is abundance, and abundance is richness.

Master Your Mind

We can't control our circumstances, but we can control our mind and how we manage the situation.

Question for you: What do you do when…

- You feel stressed, depressed, alone, anxious, or overwhelmed about….
- You wonder if there is hope for what you are going through.

Please write your answers down on the Investment Page, or on a piece of paper.

Moments when you don't feel at ease, it's very pleasing and relaxing, for the mind, to put your thoughts on paper. Writing things down can be a release and helps clear your mind. You can always throw the piece of paper away; you don't need to keep it if you don't want to. The exercise of writing your thoughts and feelings down is another way to take charge of your mind.

Setbacks or life problems can clutter your mind and make you feel like your emotions are all over the place. It is important to clear your mind because, without a clear mind, you make it harder on yourself to make sound decisions. Now, the question you might ask is, "How do you master your mind when you are constantly being challenged, and the world seems to demand so much from you?" In past years, I have advised clients to seek *the quiet place*. When things get too much for me, especially when I am overwhelmed, I always seek *the quiet* place. If it wasn't for *the quiet place*, I would have gone mental and ended up in a mental institution.

The quiet place is a place where you come to rest; this special place could be anywhere form your bedroom to out in nature. Here are some practical strategies you could adopt to help you stay in the driver's seat, no matter what comes your way.

Where to find *the quiet place:*

- Take a stroll on the beach, or a long walk in the park.
- Drive to a quiet place (only if it is safe and you are capable of driving).
- Go to your bedroom or spare room in the house.
- Sit in the garden or the garage.
- Be creative and find your own special place.

What to do in *the quiet place:*

There are only two rules for *the quite place,* and these are:

1. NO NEGATIVE THINKING!

Positive thinking
will let you do everything better
than negative thinking will.
Positive thinking
will let you use the ability
that you have,
and that is awesome.
– Zig Ziglar

2. ONLY FOCUS ON YOUR DREAMS AND GOALS

Think forward, and flip everything to the positive side —positive reinforcement is an encouragement factor that will lift your spirit.

The quiet place is for you to:
- Rejuvenate, and feel refreshed;
- Find your strength, hope, and faith;
- Pray and meditate (be still and listen to what your heart is saying);
- Read and listen to words of encouragement.
- Gratitude—take time to be thankful for what you have, and include the people in your life.
- Music is therapeutic—listen to quiet, relaxation music, such as instrumental—something to motivate you to get into the moment; relax your body, mind, and soul.

Breathing Exercise:

Stop, pause, and focus on your breathing for a moment. You can do this by putting this book down; take a moment, and close your eyes. Make sure your posture is straight while you do this exercise, and only focus on your breathing, repeatedly inhaling and exhaling slowly.

1. Take a long, slow breath in through your nose for 4 seconds, first filling your lower lungs, then your upper lungs.
2. Hold your breath to the count of "four."
3. Exhale slowly out through the mouth for four seconds, while you relax the muscles in your face, shoulders, and stomach. Repeat this technique 6 times minimum.

Breathing exercises are great for relaxation; it will settle and connect your body, and redirect you mind back to the present. Now, this can be done at any time or place, on any given day, especially when you are overwhelmed.

Exchange Setbacks for Winning

Please write your breathing experience on the Investment Page.

The quiet place is where:
- More dreams are born; more creative ideas are developed.
- You discover more of who you truly are, what you like, and what you don't want.
- You are encouraged to look beyond your ability and maximize your potential.

How often do I need to seek *the quiet place*?

Every day! You can choose to do it whenever it pleases you—morning, afternoon, or evening—it's all up to you. Some of my clients prefer to do it in the morning, as it gives them a great start for the day. If you're not a morning person, you can do it in the evening and reflect on how your day went. It is really up to you and what you feel comfortable with. Just make sure you seek the quiet place every day; this will be a benefit to you in the long run. You might find it uncomfortable at first if you have never done something like this before. Don't give up; keep trying, and eventually you'll get used to it. You can start with just ten minutes and increase the time as you go.

You are meant to be doing what you love.
Don't get distracted by setbacks.

Investment Page
Please write your experience of *the quiet place,* on the Investment Page.

I am sure you have been dying to know what the main secret to your exchange is. What is it, really, that can benefit you to live the prosperous life you have always wanted? Let's not waste more time. Turn the page, and find out in the next chapter.

Be Aware

Investment Page

_____

_____

_____

_____

_____

_____

_____

_____

_____

_____

_____

_____

_____

_____

_____

_____

CHAPTER 4

The Secret to Your Exchange

The Ancient Secret

Up to this point, you understand that the discipline of the mind is in relation with your emotions and perception. The way you view things is very important as it determines your actions and attitude. Once you're aware of what is going on, you are able to bring change into the situation.

A prosperous life will not just come your way. You will have to get it yourself. You are the solution to your success, and I'll show you what strategy you need, starting from this chapter. Several studies have shown that almost anything greatly obtained, is done through the application of a strategy.

I want to introduce you to a technique called, *Turn or Switch Your Focus Towards Others*, and I will be using this term throughout this book.

All great influencers from the past, and today, understand the link between exchanging setbacks with the winning aspect. If you could meet some of them in person, I know, without a doubt, they would all say the following to you: "Turn your focus from yourself towards others; through that, you'll find out your potential and purpose in life." I share some of their stories with you in the later chapters; but for now, let's learn more about this concept.

Turning Your Focus

It was the third time I had read Mrs. Withly's file: a 45-year-old woman with a foot injury eight years ago, and since then, she had not been able to work. Her ankles had swollen over the course of time, and standing or sitting for too long has now become a problem. The pain had limited her ability to do the things she used to enjoy. Some nights were easier than others, but a bad night implied insomnia, a tingling feeling throughout her body, and agony in both ankles. "Why can we not approve the surgery?" I thought to myself. Her surgery request had been denied twice, and here I am, the lucky one—I get to deliver the bad news. I took a deep breath and picked up the phone.

"Hello, Mrs. Withly; it's Cynthia here, from the insurance company. Do you have time to talk?"

"Yes, I do," she said.

"Mrs. Withly, I am afraid to tell you, we can't approve your surgery request. After investigating your medical reports and meetings with the physicians, it is concluded that your surgery request is unnecessary and considered not reasonable. However, we can approve further pain treatments and physiotherapy for the next 2 months."

"This is the third time I have been denied from having this surgery. I need this surgery as the pain in my ankles is unbearable. I cannot work with these ankles. There is no employment for me," she said, crying.

I gave her space and allowed her to cry and talk. I felt that she needed to be heard and acknowledged, and this went on for almost ten minutes. Once she calmed down, I said, "Mrs. Withly, once again, I am very sorry to say that the insurance company cannot help you with your request. But what I can do is give you a call 3 times a week, for 5 minutes, to check to see how you are doing. How does that sound?"

"That's very nice of you, Cynthia, and I will appreciate that," she said, in a brittle and breathy voice.

"I also believe you can play a part and do something too."

"What do you mean?" she asked quietly.

The Secret to Your Exchange

"I know you said that there is no employment for you, but what I want to suggest is for you to do some volunteer work in your community, and see how that goes. This will motivate you to engage with others, and will utilize your skills again."

"Hmm, me volunteering?" she asked.

"Yes!" I said. "Let's try that and see how it goes."

After I hung up the phone, I had a good feeling that Mrs. Withly was going to be okay. I knew that if Mrs. Withly turned her focus towards the outside world, things would change for her, and her pain in her body, and especially in her ankle, would reduce. The mind controls everything and is interchangeable with your perception. Thus, how you focus on your circumstances is how the sensors in your body will respond. After two weeks of calling Mrs. Withly, I was so pleased to hear an enthusiastic voice on the phone saying that she found a job. "You found what?" I said in a giggling voice.

"The place where I was volunteering asked me to work twice a week."

"Ah, that sounds so great, Mrs. Withly; and I am very happy for you."

"You were right, Cynthia; things have changed, and I am feeling much better. The pain in my ankles is less. I think physio is helping this time, and I am not having any disruptive nights."

"What wonderful news, Mrs. Withly; I am glad things are now working out for you."

What happened to Mrs. Withly wasn't a surprise to me, but what I didn't expect was that things changed for her very quickly: two weeks only. Witnessing miraculous changes in clients' lives, and being a believer in the concept of turning ones focus towards others through giving—the act of service and kindness—I had no doubt about the prospects in Mrs. Withly's endeavor.

BENEFITS of switching your focus:

- It motivates you to strive for your goals and dreams.
- Your perception is enlarged.

- You discover other potentials you were not aware of.
- It gives you insight, and it creates clarity.

RESULT: You feel good internally because you served another person, and you changed or impacted their life.

Look Beyond Your Circumstance

From memory, I was very nervous and uncertain, and I didn't know what to expect when my mother told me that we were going on holiday's for a month to Ghana. At that time, it had been 15 years since I left the motherland. I was only five when I left and did not know when I would return.

I received the warmest welcoming from the Ghanaians; I was overshadowed with their kindness, generosity, and exceptional hospitality.

One particular night, I decided to go for a walk with my cousin. On the way back to the house, I saw something that I had never seen before. I saw a group of people facing one direction; they were cheering, talking, shouting, and laughing. As we got closer, it appeared that someone had put their T.V. outside on a stand for the neighbors to watch. I can't remember what match they were watching, but there was a great sense of atmosphere. Instantly, I felt lively because of what I saw, and I was dazzled. It was amazing to see, how happy these people were, laughing and eating together. I thought, "These people don't have much, yet one of them decided to share what they had so that anyone could join the wealth of one man. And not only that, but the choice made by one man, to share, brought the community together.

When we reached home, I couldn't stop thinking about what I saw, and I kept questioning myself, "How can they be so genuinely happy, yet they don't have much?" The western world would say these people were poor, but in my eyes, they are extremely rich. They had more because their mind had equipped them to be content with one another. They didn't have many material things, but they had each other, and their community. What I witnessed that day left me with more questions. While still thinking about them, I thought, "With no abundance of resources and materials, their circumstances had pushed them to turn their focus from themselves to others. Spending time with one another had not only become a custom but also had given them happiness. As a result, their minds were in a better state. Life is truly all about relationships and bringing more fulfillment. I would say they were definitely rich in spirit. This is how they lived! Their focus was on each other, on other people, and not on their circumstances." I believe they would have been cheerless if their focus had been on their circumstances, and if they were troubled by life pressures. In comparison, from the Western world's point of view, it would seem as if they wouldn't be able to cope due to the insufficient resources and materials. This insight led me to the next thought, "The Western world has more materials and resources, yet some rich folks are not happy at all. When I was young, I thought rich people were always happy; I believed they could buy anything they wanted. Obviously, I know by now that money is not everything."

While Tony Robbins was conducting research on rich people's happiness, surprisingly, he said that a large amount of the wealthiest people in this world are not truly happy. Yet again, money is not the solution to happiness. The Ghanians I saw on that day taught me an important lesson, and it confirmed my grandmother's wise words too: *To live is to give*. Be careful not to be consumed with your own world or to look too much in your own world, but invite others into your world. *True happiness is found in the closeness and in the company of others. It has more meaning when it is shared with those around you.* To give love, to receive love, and to share love is priceless. No money can buy love, as love does not have a price tag. When you give, you make a personal statement, where you say, "Love is a choice, and I choose you."

Love is when you choose to understand and to see the value in another person.

Now I Understand

The future awaits me, and my full potential has not been uncovered yet. I am on a quest of discovering my gifts and talents, one by one. There is nothing that can stop me now. Life challenges might pull me from everywhere, left and right, but I have made the promise to myself not to be distracted but to keep my eyes on what I hope to see. I believe I have something extraordinary to offer to the world. I now understand that I am on a journey of exchanging my value with the world—my world—the people I share my life with, my friends, my family, my colleagues, my community, and anyone who crosses my path. I am ready to give what I love and enjoy doing: that gift that makes me look good, and gives me confidence and a sense of fulfillment. The knowledge I have, the way I speak and explain how things work, nobody can present their gift the way I do. I am ready to exchange my value with others. When I add value to my gift, I exchange my gifts to serve others. And that act makes me valuable. I am not afraid to exchange because I now understand that the person, the community, and the world I am exchanging with, are also giving their best.

This, N*ow I Understand* affirmation is for you and me. Say this regularly, especially when you feel like you need to be reconnected with yourself again.

Keep the Value

While growing up, my grandmother taught me to see the best in every person, and to give people the benefit of the doubt. "Give them the opportunity to prove their best to you, Cynthia," I remember her saying. "You will meet people who will disappoint you; you will feel pain and want to protect yourself. When you change, or close up and don't give anyone the chance to get to know who you truly are, you then unconsciously give power to people to change you. Cynthia, never change who you are for anybody," she said. I was very young when she said those words. I had no Idea what she was talking about until it hit me, at the age of 17.

People I was hanging out with at that time were breaking their promises, lying, and not following through with their words. I guess, at that age, I was still naive to believe that I could trust people in general. At one point, I thought, "I am not going to lend any of my stuff, such as books or CD's, to people anymore." I started putting barriers and walls up, and became very skeptical of people. Luckily, this behavior of mine was only for a short time. I noticed the change in me, and I hated who I was becoming. I remember feeling very different and unhappy with myself. I felt so mean to people, and I knew that wasn't me. At that point, I heard my grandmother's voice in my head and remembered what she said. I then made a promise to myself not to change who I am. To limit myself in serving people would mean permitting others to change me into a different person. *To suppress who I am is an exclusion—as if I was never born.* You should never be invisible—make sure you count! Your sense of worth equals your value. Do whatever you can to witness what you can become. You will not know until you test your own ability. Try it! Work hard and pay the price, and receive your reward in value. We all must take the responsibility to ignite our value. While we are all exchanging our value with each other, each of us receives an inexplicable return.

You give your best to receive the best.

Exchange Setback for Wining

Entrepreneur, life coach, philanthropist, bestselling author, life and business strategist: Tony Robbins. The founder of several companies, with a profit of approximately 6 billion in annual sales, Tony has impacted many lives over the last 40 years.

Tony opened the door to success at the age of 18, with the principle, *living is giving*. Too early to dictate his success, he took the courage to exchange his setback for winning. Little did he know what would happen, when he decided to turn his focus from himself to a

Exchange Setbacks for Winning

nine-year-old boy.

At that time, Tony was broke and only had $21 to his name. For weeks he had been trying to get hold of a friend who had borrowed money from him. Tony's desperation led him to calling the guy ten times. He felt sorry for himself as the guy was not returning his calls. He hoped to use that money to pay his overdue rent, and to buy some groceries because he was starving.

Walking into an all-you-can-eat salad bar, he picked out the cheapest dish. While Tony was eating, a little boy, dressed in his little vest and suit (age 9 or 10), walked in with his beautiful mother. The boy had outstanding manners: he opened the door, pulled out the chair for his mother, and then they sat down. The boy's attention was 100% on the mother. This moved Tony and made him walk up to the boy. "Hi, I am Tony."

"Hi, am Paul." (Today Tony can't remember the little boy's name, so he calls him Paul.)

Tony continued, "You are a class act. I saw you hold the door open for your woman. I saw you pull out the chair for her. Taking her out for lunch like that, that is really cool."

"She is my mom", Paul said.

"That's even cooler. Take her to lunch," Tony said, with a smile on his face.

Paul goes, "Well, I didn't take her to lunch. I'm nine years old, and I don't have a job yet."

"Yes, you are taking her to lunch," Tony said, while reaching in his pocket. Tony dropped $17 in front of Paul and walked out of the salad bar.

Standing outside, he realized that he had nothing left in his pocket—he gave it all. As he inhaled the fresh air with closed eyes, he felt no fear, no scarcity. He thought to himself, "This is the most powerful experience of my life." When he reached home, he repeated to himself again, "I have no money now. I have no money. Nothing!"

The very next day, he found a letter in his letter box. It was a letter from the guy he had lent money to. With resentment and hurt, Tony opened the letter. "Dear Tony, I am really sorry. I know you have been trying to reach me. I've been avoiding you. Here's the money I owe, and I'm going to give you some interest as well." Tony could not believe what he was reading. Now he had more money than yesterday: $1200.

With the letter still in his hands, overwhelmed with the miracle, I am letting Tony finish the story for you.

"I'm sitting there, tears running down my face. I'm an emotional character. I chose to believe—I don't know if it's true—but I chose to believe that it's because I let go of just trying to take care of myself. I did what was right. Life's not about me; it's about *we*. That's also why, when people are suffering, it's always because you're obsessing about yourself. You're obsessing that something happened, and now you have less. You think you have less. Or something happened and you've lost something: lost love, lost money, lost significance, lost attention, lost something.

When you are in a state of suffering—this obsession with self—you can snap out of it. All you have to do is stop expecting, and start appreciating. If you're going to wait till you think you're going to have something, you're never going to have something of any size or scope. There's something inside the human psyche that when you do what's right, and you get out of yourself, there's something that'll click for you. So, it's a long way of saying, when you have nothing is when you need to get something."

I hope you are inspired by Tony's story and are starting to believe in this ancient secret of life.

To stretch out and get involved in the lives of others is the most rewarding aspect of life. To make a difference in somebody's life is another life's blueprint. This secret has been evidential, and has been used over many centuries and decades, by various people from all walks of life. Some find it earlier than others, and some never find it. You reading this book means you have the secret to a prosperous life, in your hands.

The secret to living is giving.

> **Investment Page**
>
> I made a promise to myself not to change who I am for anyone; what about you?
>
> - How do you maintain your value?
> - Do you remember a time when you turned your focus from yourself, like Mrs. Withly and Tony?
>
> Write your answers on the Investment Page.

You are going to be amazed about the next chapter! Finally, you will have a better understanding about your purpose in life. You invest in others by first finding out your value. If you don't know what you've got, you can't give it. To find out, we will be looking at 3 major qualities, which involves 3 steps:

1. Who you are
2. What you are meant to be doing (your purpose)
3. What your gifts and talents are

The Secret to Your Exchange

Investment Page

CHAPTER 5

Let's Check Out Your Investment

Know Your Value

How you see yourself is everything. And what you believe about yourself is also everything.

What you believe internally about yourself is how you portray yourself from the outside. How you view yourself is how you allow someone to treat you. You might not have been aware of it. You have to first start believing in yourself, then the rest will follow you—they will line up with you and believe in you. You can assess yourself by paying more attention to your interactions with people. This includes your behavior and daily communication. You might notice how people react or give you feedback.

We all know that no one, and I mean no one, is replaceable. Nobody is like you, has the exact personality, characteristics, generosity, gifts, and talents as you. You are unique, one of a kind, special, genuine, an extraordinary person. You are a high value person (HVP); no one can do you, and there is only ONE of YOU.

I hope you are starting to see yourself as a valuable person, and hopefully, you believe that too.

Don't Be Afraid to Shine

In reality, the world is there for you to take, and it belongs to each and every one of us. It is so large that there is plenty of room for each of us to shine. But for some reason, because of our poor belief system, and what you and I have accumulated over the years, we do not always have the courage to do what we really want to do. The thought of doing what I really want, or what people thought of me, was sometimes a battlefield in my mind. How many times have I wondered if I could achieve something? But during moments like this, I remember what my mother thought me. While growing up, she always said, "Cynthia, it does not matter what you do; you will always have a cheering audience and an audience that boos. If that is the case, you might as well do what you want. There is nothing that you can't do or possibly can't have."

I had to learn this concept, and I am still learning to take myself to a higher level of achieving more and more. Another time in my life, I realized that I had not achieved some of my dreams due to poor self-image. Had I known what I know today, I would have reached some of my dreams at an earlier stage of my life. On the other hand, all my experiences have taken me to this point. It has not been counted as lost but a learning curve and triumph. It's all about your perception; life has so much to offer. You and I can easily be blinded because of our poor beliefs about ourselves. In all honesty, there are some people who are enjoying and loving what they do. It seems like they have discovered their mark in life along the way, or at an early stage of their life. They tapped into their high valued person mindset and didn't let anything change their mind—rather, they received the best that life had to offer them. I would like to share with you one of my favorite poems, *Our Deepest Fear*, written by Marianne Williamson.

"Our deepest fear is not that we are inadequate. Our deepest fear is that we are powerful beyond measure. It is our light, not our darkness that most frightens us. We ask ourselves, who am I to be brilliant, gorgeous, talented, fabulous? Actually, who are you not to be? You are a child of God. Your playing small does not serve the world. There's nothing enlightened about shrinking so that other people won't feel insecure around you. We are all meant to shine, as children do. We were born to make manifest the glory of God that is within us. It's not just in some of us; it's in everyone. And as we let our own light shine, we unconsciously give other people permission to do the same. As we're liberated from our own fear, our presence automatically liberates others."

    YOU are the treasure in this world! Every person has a desire and strong will power that is connected to their gifts and talents. It is your responsibility to find your treasure that is YOU, and once you find your treasure, you teach others to find theirs.
    Do not let anyone tell you that you cannot have what life has to offer you. Not everyone will have the same knowledge, understanding, or will power as you. They might be in fear, at a different stage of their life, or don't believe in this concept we have discussed so far. Never get discouraged, but get the maximum out of life. Just because you have not seen your life fulfilled yet does not mean there is nothing out there for you. There is greatness within you, and so much greatness waiting for you, that you have not seen yet. I will say to be open: open your mind, open your eyes, open your heart, and open your hands. Have a go! And challenge yourself; see what life has to offer you. Do not limit yourself, whatever you are looking for; it's in you and already out there for you. Believe!
    To maximize your world view and sense of worth, you will have to make continuous bold and visionary decisions. I hope you are starting to see and believe that you are a high valued person (HVP) and that you have whatever it takes. If you struggle with this concept, then I would like for you to take up the challenge. Believe that you are a HVP, apply what I have said so far, and you will witness some positive changes this year.
    Or you can choose to stay where you are and still believe that you are just an average person. I warn you though, if you choose not to take up the challenge, you will miss out on the total package of why you are here and what you're meant to be doing for yourself. But I know you are eager to bring positive change in your life; otherwise, you would not be reading this book. Moreover, I believe you want an extraordinary life, and you don't tolerate a mediocre lifestyle.

Shine your light and show us the way!

Trust Your Instinct

Let's say you don't feel quite fulfilled, or believe there is more to your life.

That strong feeling of knowing that there is more, and that you are supposed to be doing something great, is a sense that each and all of us carry with us.

Personally, this is the stage where I am myself. I looked back from the time when I was young, as far back as I could remember. In the first vision, I saw myself traveling abroad, first to one country, and then visiting to many more different countries. Then I saw myself speaking multiple languages at important places, advocating for those who don't have a voice. I saw myself comforting children all over the world, of different nationalities and places. I saw myself standing up for justice and helping people from all walks of life. My heart always goes out to people who are in need. I want to see children, youth, families, and individuals live a high quality of life. At a young age, I saw myself living a luxurious lifestyle in a warm country, where English was the first language spoken. I saw my name on published books, and being an author, artist, and photographer. At the age of 21, while on holiday in Ghana, I saw a child on the street. I will guess she was 8 years old. She was walking by herself, and her dress was slightly filthy and torn. She was by herself, and I did not understand; I hoped for her not to be an orphan. As I walked past her, I questioned myself, "Why was I taken away from this place? Was I fortunate? Or was I taken away and had to be brought back for a cause?"

It is not that Ghana doesn't have many opportunities for an individual to excel, but living in the western world has slightly more opportunities for the average person. At that moment, I strongly believed that I had to return and give something back—whether or not it was to support some orphanages—in a way to say a simple thank you to the place where I came from. My desire grew, and I wanted to help. I wanted to be able to give children who face disadvantages a chance or opportunities to discover their purpose in life.

* I have shared some of my instincts with you. What are yours? What is your belief telling you? Write your answers on the Investment Page or in your notebook.

The Goal

To be fulfilled, content, and truly happy, you will need to discover:

- Who You Are
- Your Purpose
- Your Potential
- Your Vision
- Your Gift

Who You Are Is Everything

I had to dig deep, find myself again, and rethink my life purpose when I hit rock bottom in 2016. I had to ask myself again who I was—it had been over 2 years since I had not felt like myself. The illness had completely changed who I was. I was afraid to go to places, as I never knew what could happen. The bleeding could start anytime, and it always came without a warning. My days and weeks were filled with doctor and hospital visits, heavy doses of meds, and iron infusion. I went through a phase where I stopped going out, and I avoided people who were not close to me. It felt better to stay away from people because it was easier not to explain what I was going through. I hated the fact that I couldn't recognize myself anymore when I looked in the mirror. Who am I?

The interesting thing is that when people are asked who they are, the majority get this question mixed up with their career. Who you are is not what you do; your job or career is separate from your true identity. You are a person living in a human body, with a soul and a spirit, and you are born with gifts, talents, and potential. To find out more about yourself, you will have to spend quality time with yourself—analyzing things you like and things you enjoy doing.

Who you are—the core, your true identity—is a journey only you can answer to. As for me, I never knew who I truly was until I started reading the Bible at age 19, and found out that I am a child of God. I don't know about you, but whatever stage you find yourself in, do whatever it takes to be grounded in yourself. Know who you are. I would say, to know who you are is 70% of your success in life. Your identity is what will make you or break you— your sanity depends on your identity. Once you know who you are, nobody can dictate your life for you—this includes setbacks. You will always rise above anything. I can't stress enough how important and satisfying it is to know who you truly are. If you ever feel stuck and want to connect with me or ask questions, please feel free to send me a direct message by going onto www.ExchangeAndWinLife.com. I will do my best to answer you, so don't be shy.

To find your way, sometimes you will get lost first.

To help you find your identity, read the following questions, which have crossed every human's mind. Some have figured it out, and others are still on a quest. Have a look at them, and see how much you know about yourself. Don't forget to write your answers on the Investment Page.

- Why are you here?
- Where are you from?
- Why were you born?
- Why are you living in this generation?
- Are your views based on what people say about you?
- Are you following the crowd, or have you chosen your own path?
- If you have chosen your own path, do you know where you are going?

Let's Check Out Your Investment

- What is your outlook?
- How do you see yourself in the next three, five, or ten years?

You might think, why all these questions, and how important are they? From my own experience, working with many clients from all walks of life, research and studies show that life without purpose is a devastation to the human soul. In order to be fulfilled, you will have to find your purpose in this life. Your **fulfillment lies in your purpose.**

Learn to know who you are, and develop yourself.

Your Purpose in Life

-Purpose-
The reason for which you were created
or for which you exist;
your sense of resolve or determination.

People, including myself, say that we are all meant to find our purpose in life, but what does it really mean? To help you understand, your existence is not an accident nor a coincidence.

You are designed to blossom to the fullest of your ability. There is a reason why you are here, and there is a reason for your existence. You are alive because you are needed in this generation. You matter! The desires you hold so dearly in your heart, which speak of your passion, is your biggest clue in life. You're meant to follow your passion; find what it entails, develop it, and persist till you see the outcome or result.

Until you have found what it is, you will always have the feeling that you're meant to do something different from what you are doing right now. To get rid of that feeling, and to be fulfilled and content in life, you will have to find your purpose.

> *"When you find purpose and meaning in what you are doing in one area of your life, it grows in every area of your life because you are one person."*
> – Dr. Robert Quinn

Potential

Once you find your purpose—knowing what you are meant to be doing here on earth—you uncover your potential.

To find your potential—what does it even mean?

As earlier mentioned in Chapter 1, the majority of us grow up believing what other people say about us. I am sure, when you were young, you believed that literally anything was possible. Your *child faith* told you that you could create anything, go anywhere, and become whatever you wanted to be. But then, you got told that big dreams do not come to pass, or you had to be realistic, and then fear crept into your life. Fear is the perfect dream killer: it teaches you not to maximize your potential. It tells you not to move forward but to stay just where you are. Moreover, the unknown freaks you out. Because you do not know how things will turn out, you back out. But hey, what if you take the step forward, and you discover something you didn't know about yourself.

I mean, the fact that you are still here means that IT is not over yet; you were born for a purpose and to make a difference. To develop, to be different, to be unique, and to stand out in the crowd, and to make yourself useful, is called *potential*.

-Potential-
Latent qualities or abilities that you may develop,
and this leads to future success or usefulness;
the possibility of you doing something great in the future.

Let's Check Out Your Investment

Potential is what you can become in the future: the YOU that no one has seen yet, including yourself. If you have not yet pushed yourself to the maximum, you don't know all the great things you possibly could become or create.

Think about all you could be, and write it down on the Investment Page.

What you see on your paper are some of your potentials. I know there is more in you. I believe there is more; there is so much more that you haven't even discovered yet. I also know for a fact that once you change your mindset and endorse all that is in this book, you will squeeze all the potential out of yourself, and I cannot wait to see that for you. I am excited for you, and for me. Why me? Because I get to enjoy and experience your gift.

Potential is the hidden treasure inside you.
-Dream Big-

While you tap into your own potential and pursue your goals and dreams, you learn to be more creative with your gifts and talents. Your life becomes productive when you stretch out your hands. Interestingly enough, while you give your best, you free and teach others to give their best too. People get inspired, motivated, and influenced by you to do the same.

Are you maximizing your full potential?

*What are your abilities, or what do you think you do BEST? Please write them down on the Investment Page.

Vision, Dreams, and Passion

A vision is a deep conviction you can't let go.

Your vision is a glimpse of your dream—some dreams could be fulfilled in a lifetime, and visions are often accomplished within a lifetime. A dream is an imagination you cannot let go, a secret treasure you hold dear, deep inside you.

Your vision will always work in your favor and develop your potential to the fullest. Your vision is your direction; it will tell you how to walk your journey. It is when you follow your vision that your dreams come true. You must believe in your vision more than the people around you, because you are the only one that can make it happen. You are the first believer when it comes to your vision. If your vision sounds crazy to others, don't worry; that is a good thing. Your crazy ideas will make you stand out from the crowd. Today, we take an airplane to cross the ocean and travel. I am sure, when the Wright brothers, Orville and Wilbur, told their friends and family, they probably said, "You must be crazy! What do you mean, flying in the air? How is that possible?"

If you want to be a person of value, you will have to live by your vision and start talking about it. The more you speak about it, the more you start believing. Plus, it will help you stay on track, and people could hold you accountable for it too. For me, accountability is an energy that drives me to accomplish what I want. It tells me that people are watching and waiting for me, and it creates a personal challenge. And please understand this: the details of your journey are not necessarily important. When you are trying something and it doesn't work out, it does not mean you failed; it means you need to find a better strategy to make it happen. The key is to finish what you've started. You only make things happen when you complete your task. *Anyone can start something great, but not everyone finishes what they start. Choose to be the one that's finishes.*

Let's Check Out Your Investment

Live by your vision; dare yourself and see how far will you go.

Dreams: a deep desire reflected in your imaginations; hope displayed in pictures that only you can see. You must have a dream; you cannot stop dreaming, and you must always keep dreaming. You are designed to be a dreamer; it is built in you. You have the ability to dream, so don't let anyone stop you. You have been dreaming since you were a child, but as you started developing, society and people discouraged you not to take your dreams seriously or to believe in them. You are a winner of life—your dreams give you hope and a meaning for existing. Hope gives you the possibility to pursue and to look out for tomorrow.

Passion is the idea you cannot stop talking about. You don't even care who is listening or not. Passion is what drives you; it will give you the reason to get up in the morning. Passion is what keeps you and your dreams connected. Passion will always give you hope and stand by your side. If you allow passion to rule your life, it will not disappoint you but will assist you in achieving your dream.

Differences Between Gifts, Talents, and Skills

A gift is a unique, natural ability, aptitude or talent.
A talent is an innovative skill that comes naturally to you.
A skill is the work, expertise, and ability to do something well.

You were born with a gift. When a gift is discovered and developed, you see talent. The ability to utilize and to practice the gift and talent is what I call the skill.

You might have been asking yourself, "How do I make myself valuable?" You make yourself valuable to the world by using your gift, talent, and skill you have—use everything!

Here are prompt questions. This should help you think in the right direction of discovering and developing your gift. Write your answers on the Investment Page.

- What are you doing already that you enjoy doing, and it just comes very naturally to you?
- What can you do? What do you believe you can do that requires minimal effort?
- What is your strength, specialty, and uniqueness?
- What would you like to share or give to your community and the world?

You have many qualities, talents, and gifts that you have been using from the time you were born until today. You might not have been recognizing them, and might have overlooked your gift. I need you to take a moment, and accept what I am about to say to you. To add value to yourself, you will have to develop your gifts and talents. Your gifts and talents are what will lead you to success, and not the other way around. So, you don't go after your success first and hope to find your gift or talent. Discover your gift first! And to stand out, your gift needs to be slightly or totally different from someone else. Once your gift is designed, it becomes valuable, and anything that has a value is rewarded with money. Plus, people will automatically give you more respect.

For example, after I graduated as a professional counsellor, I looked for a job in the school of psychology. While trying to find a place in the market, I found it to be very competitive. What I did then was to get myself an Applied Behavior Analysis certificate. This provided me with a license to specialize in the disability sector. At the completion of all my degrees, I had the title, *Professional Counsellor, Specializing in Applied Behavior Analysis*. With that credential, I was able to start a private practice for families and children, youth, and autistic individuals, providing counseling and behavior analysis. The combination of counseling, psychology, and behavior analysis is very rare, and clients were so happy when they found me. I tailored my gift to serving people of a certain group, who are in need of my service. Could you believe that clients didn't want to be referred when I decided to stop the private practice? They all communicated, saying that it took them a while to find me because my service is uncommon.

Let's Check Out Your Investment

I can see why my clients were happy with me: the service brought a solution to their need.

I challenge you to believe in your talents, gifts, and qualities, more than you ever have before. Start today.

> *Discover your gift*
> *Develop your gift*
> *Then YOU and your GIFT*
> *Will be recognized by others*

Learn To Say NO

At some point in our lives, we all wonder what our next step would be, "Where to go from here?"

Perhaps…

You are confused and you're trying to find out your purpose and dreams in life.

You thought you would have reached your dreams and goals by now, but you have not.

You are trying to pursue your dreams and goals, but it seems far away—it's a struggle.

Every so often, you would have to take on the attitude of a three-year-old child. Seriously, you do; I am not joking. Clients I've worked with have found it helpful to use the three-year- old strategy. A three-year-old child loves to say, "NO," to everything they don't like. They totally abuse the word, *no*, until mom and dad realize that their three-year-old child is just taking advantage of the new word learned: "NO!" Learn to say no, and it will benefit you and eliminate commitments that are not aligned with your goals. You will find more time to invest in yourself.

Here is a simple way to start:

- Take time to brainstorm—ask yourself first **what you truly want,** and be honest in your approach; move then to the "how" question: how you can reach your goals?
- Take time to think through how you can work smarter, and refuse to work yourself to death.
- Take time to exercise, to eat healthy, and get quality sleep.
- Take time for self-development. Get familiar with the resources that are out there, and use that to your advantage.
- Take time to be creative, to come up with new ideas—be innovative.
- Take time to seek professional support for areas where you know you can't do it on your own.
- Take time to go on holidays, as this can revive and give you more strength to progress.
- Take time for gratitude.
- Take time to think about your ideal career. In Chapters 5, 6, and 7, you will learn to identify your gifts. For now, I want to share a few ideas.

You are the only one who can correct yourself, avoid distractions, and choose to stay focused.

Don't let life challenges take away what you love or enjoy doing. I am sure you wouldn't let anyone come to your house and take your new TV, your favorite couch, or your best pair of shoes. What I am trying to say is to have the same temper, and take responsibility for your purpose here on earth. I also had to learn to say no; otherwise, you wouldn't be reading this book. At the end of last year, I looked back on the year 2017, and the years before, and I realized how much time had gone by—I felt robbed. I questioned myself, "Cynthia, who robbed you? No one, really," I thought. I had allowed myself to be distracted by all that had happened in that year. Time had flown by. I didn't deposit enough time in ME, but more in other stuff, which had now taken me further away. It was shocking to think that I had allowed myself to be distracted. Plus, I was annoyed with the amount of time I wasted—watching Netflix, shopping, going out, and spending hours on my phone.

Coming from the bottom of my heart, learn from my mistakes and make changes; choose to invest in YOU, and give yourself the best that life has to offer you. It is more than what you already have or can gain.

Let me know how it goes, and please send an email to www.ExchangeAndWinLife.com, as I would like to hear how you are doing.

Moving forward, pay attention to your setbacks, and don't be fooled or carried away. You can't let life's problems follow you for years; take responsibility and get rid of them as soon as you can. Learn to say, "No!" without negativity! Cool? I think I heard you saying YES!

Say YES only to the things you love and enjoy.

Don't Die With the Dream

You have either found yourself doing what you love doing, and if so, you are on the right track; or, you are not sure about what you want, and you are still searching. Whatever phase of life you are in, I hope the following will stir the dream in you even more.

Once, Dr. Myles Munroe, international bestselling author, lecturer, teacher, leadership mentor, life coach, business and government consultant, shared that the most wealthiest place on earth is the graveyard.

I thought to myself, "Why?"

"The people are dead and gone. They died with their potential, and it's all buried away in the ground," he explained. What a tragedy! The bestselling book was never written; the best song was never written or sang; the best design was never created; the best artwork was never displayed; the best music was never created; the best entrepreneur is unknown; the best innovation or technology product will never be seen by anyone; the best company, bakery shop,

Exchange Setbacks for Winning

restaurant, or cafe was never opened; the best comedian, photographer, journalist, speaker, actor or actress, chiropractor or director—whatever it was—no one ever saw. I could go on forever, and this book will then end with all the possibility of the treasures you and I could have witnessed too.

What is it that you have inside you? The hidden treasures in you—will you die with your dream, or will you share your dreams with me and the rest of the world? Will some of us ever see you fulfilling your dreams? You have many ideas that you keep thinking about, and those thoughts seem to not let you go. My question to you is, what do you do with them? Do you push them away? Perhaps your reason might be fear, or you don't know how to start, and as a result, you ignore your vision, or you just keep pushing it away. You keep talking about it, but there is no action behind your words. If you step back and listen to yourself, you will hear that you are often sharing your deepest desire. The fact that you're speaking about it means you already know the *how*—where to start from. You probably have done some research about it, purely because of interest. The only thing left is the actions behind your words. This might sound funny or silly, but maybe you should record yourself once you start talking about your ideas, and then write them down. All you need to do is to grab your phone—today, most smart phones have a recording function. Another thing is that when you are talking to people, friends, and family about your ideas and dreams, you are spontaneous, relaxed, excited, and not worried at all. Pay attention next time when you speak about the secrets of your heart.

Don't leave this place with your potential; leave it for others.

Let's Check Out Your Investment

Investment Page

- Have you been distracted?
- Do you recognize the stumbling blocks?
- What was your initial plan—your destination—your destiny?

Write your answers on the Investment Page.

I am thrilled for you to read the next chapter. You will find out how some well-known, successful people exchange their setbacks for winning.

Exchange Setbacks for Winning

Investment Page

CHAPTER 6

Let People Be Your Inspiration

You can only influence others when you invest in yourself first.

I have been inspired by many successful people; they helped me to look beyond myself. They told me not to be afraid but to look fear in the eye. They taught me a lesson that has stuck with me for life: "Cynthia, if you work hard and devote all your time to what you want, it is guaranteed that you will succeed." Their influence in my life made it easier to believe in the possibilities. They proved to me that anything is truly possible as long as you set your mind to it. You can do and become anything you want, with hard work and perseverance. When you follow your passion or dream, you will make mistakes, and that's okay. The key is to learn from your mistakes, to do it better next time, and never to give up on your dream. Nobody has ever gained something from giving up.

I hope sharing their stories with you will have the same effect or greater impact on your life.

You will read about how most influential people started with nothing: they used what they had, and took small and big steps to turn their lives around. They refused to stay at the stage they were at. They took courage, and with a vision in mind, they made their success inevitable. They all exchanged their setbacks for winning, despite their odds.

"If I tell you all the people who told me I wasn't going to act or sing or dance, or I wasn't good at it, or I should stop or I should quit, or even after I became famous for doing these things, that I would be locked in a house somewhere doing nothing. The truth is, nobody knows what's inside of you. Only you know what's inside of you. Only you know what you can accomplish, what you're capable of, and what your gut tells you, and your dreams and your desires and your wants and your ability—only you know. Nobody else knows. Whatever you feel in your heart and in your gut, you should follow that. Follow that. Then if that changes one day, that's fine too. Then you follow that. You're the only one who knows. Nobody else."
– Jennifer Lopez

Whether music and playing an instrument is your passion or not, be encouraged by the following career starting point.

Did you know...?

A friend of Adele posted a demo of Adele's on Myspace, shortly after Adele graduated from BRIT School. Adele then received a phone call from Richard Russel, and received her first contract from XL Recordings. (Adele Adkins: singer and songwriter)

Blind since birth, Stevie Wonder signed with Motown's Tamla label, at an audition at age 11. (Stevie Wonder: singer, songwriter, record producer, and multi-instrumentalist)

Alicia Keys, at age 16, followed her passion and dropped out of Columbia University to pursue her music career full-time. (Alicia Keys: singer, songwriter, pianist, music producer, philanthropist, and actress)

Justin Bieber's mother placed a video of him singing on YouTube. He was then discovered by a talent manager, who signed Justin to RBMG. (Justin Bieber: singer, songwriter, and actor)

Madonna lost her mother at a young age. The change caused a sequence of setbacks in her life. She dropped out of college, moved to New York City with only $35, and worked as a waitress. After moving to NYC, she was held at knifepoint and raped. Not allowing the major setback to stop her, she started taking dance classes and became a backup dancer for popular artists. As time went on, she quickly learned to write songs, and shortly after, she decided to go solo. DJ and record producer, Mark Gamins, noticed Madonna's work, introduced her to Sire Records founder, Seymour, and she received her first singles deal. (Madonna: singer, songwriter, actress, businesswoman, record producer, dancer, film director, author, and humanitarian)

Sting was a teacher before becoming a singer. During the college breaks, he performed jazz in the evening and on the weekends. Things skyrocketed in 1977, when he joined the band, The Police. His first solo album was in 1985. (Stage name Sting, Gordon Summer: singer, musician, songwriter, and actor)

Whatever you are working on, make sure you put it out there. There is no point in keeping it. Share what you've got, to receive your reward in respect and money.

KFC – Colonel Sanders

The first time I had KFC was with my friend, Kim, in Amsterdam. I can't remember how old we were, but I will say 15 or 16. With the biggest smile I had ever seen on Kim's face, she said, "Cynthia, I need to take you to this chicken place. It's really good, and I want you to try it. I am taking you today after school, and you're coming!"

"Okay," I said. I had no idea what to expect. Standing at the entrance, with a giggling and merry voice, Kim says, "This is the place; it's called Kentucky Fried Chicken, and it's on me. The moment I took my first bite, I thought, "Kim is right! This chicken is amazing!"

(Colonel Sanders: entrepreneur; founder of KFC, the world's most popular fast food chain, and fourth largest restaurant, with over 20,000 locations.) Raised in poverty, Colonel's global success did not start until the age of sixty-six. His triumph came about when most people are about to retire. If anyone had a determined spirit, it would be Colonel, who lost his hard working father at the age of five. He helped his hardworking mother raise his 2 younger siblings. His

Exchange Setbacks for Winning

mother also taught him to cook, as this was needed while looking after his siblings. Colonel took the father's role upon himself early, started the workforce at the age of 10, and quit school to work full-time.

He had various jobs, such as a painter, conductor, and soldier, by the age of 17. He then took the challenge further by working as a cleaner, blacksmith, and fireman, and then studied law and worked as legal counsellor. As a representor of railroad workers, Colonel's job did not last long. He quickly moved on to selling insurance and Michelin tires, and again, he was let go. He got married at 18, and at age 20, his wife left him, with their baby daughter. With all these setbacks, he never gave up. He opened a gas station six years later, where he sold fried chicken to hungry commuters along the highway.

While trying different delicious seasoning recipes, his cooking skills seemed to come in handy at this point. His Kentucky-fried chicken stood out the most for the hungry travelers. This led him to open a restaurant across the street. At the age of 50, his secret, 11-blend seasoned chicken became more and more popular. In honor and respect, he received the name, Kentucky Colonel, by the state governor. Soon after World War 2 took place, Colonel had to close the restaurant down. You would think this was the end, but no, with an incredible non-defeated mentality, he was not settling for anything less.

"I was sixty-six years old. I still had to make a living. I looked at my social security check of 105 dollars and decided to use that to franchise my chicken recipe. Folks had always liked my chicken."

Going from diners to restaurants, introducing his recipe, cooking just enough to get by, and sleeping in the back of his car, he was denied 1009 times before being given a chance. The first Kentucky Fried Chicken franchise was opened in 1952. With booming success, and over 600 franchise outlets, Colonel sold KFC to investors for 2 million (today, this would be more than 15 million), at age 73.

Colonel's inspiring story encourages you and me to never give up, and it is never too late to start anything, regardless of your age. He was sixty-six years old! No matter how life has treated you so far, or what childhood struggles you may have had, your setbacks can be the

Let People Be Your Inspiration

stepping stone to your future. Keep imagining, and don't let your past define your future success. As long as you don't let go of your determination, passion, and vision, there is nothing you can't do. You can do anything!

"I've only had two rules. Do all you can, and do it the best you can. It's the only way you ever get that feeling of accomplishing something."
– Colonel Sanders

*Do you remember your first time when you had KFC? Where were you, and with whom? To see a full-sized, colored picture of Kim—the friend I had my first KFC experience with—go to www.ExchangeAndWinLife.com.

Tyler Perry

"I ended up homeless. I ended up out in the street with no money and nothing to my name. But my intention was just to make enough money to be able to take care of my mother. That's all I wanted to do. That was my goal."
– Tyler Perry

Abused by his father, Tyler's childhood was not always easy. While going through a long period of rough times, Tyler's defining moment was not until he heard Oprah Winfrey saying on television that writing your thoughts and feelings down can bring healing and make you feel better. Tyler took Oprah's advice and started journalizing. He then transformed some of his journal stories into successful plays and shows. Today, Tyler also produces movies and carries the title of actor, director, and writer.

Tyler inspires the following: *"How you grow up does not have to determine your future. As long as you have a goal, a vision, or a deep need to change your situation, you will have success."*

Dwayne Johnson
Hollywood actor, Dwayne Johnson, also known as the Rock

My father was a professional wrestler, and so was my grandfather. Dad worked really hard to put food on the table and, as a wrestler, he was often on the road. As the years went by, I saw my dad less and less; it was only Mom and I at home. When he was around, he would argue with Mom, and this was not getting less either. The disruption and tension at home caused me to get into fights at school; so frequently that the police were called on numerous occasions. On top of that, we were doing really bad financially, and this lead Mom and Dad to divorce. One day, when I was 14 years old, Mom found a padlock and an eviction notice taped on our door. I remember that day; I felt helpless as I watched my mother break down crying. I felt depressed, as we had nowhere to go and did not know where we would sleep. Luckily, our family lent us 1 week's rent to re-rent our home. That night, lying in bed, I thought, "How can I keep this from happening again? I never want to see my mother like that again." I was so grateful that I was saved from sleeping outside; I was thankful to sleep in my bed. That same night, I thought of my two heroes: Stallone and Schwarzenegger. I wanted to be like them and be successful.

I started to train hard, and I enrolled at Freedom High School in Pennsylvania, at the age of 16. One of my teachers introduced me to football, and I fell in love with it. Football helped me to slowly get out of the deep depression I had been going through. At 18, I won a full scholarship from the University of Miami, to play defensive tackle. I started to dream again, and believed that I would be an NFL player one day. Unfortunately, I was having multiple injuries, which held me back. I slipped into deep depression again, and dropped out. Thanks to my coach at that time, I went back to university and graduated with a criminology degree. I then moved to Canada to pursue my dream of becoming an NFL player. I was broke at this stage and survived on Ramen noodles. When I was cut from the team after two months, I was shattered. I felt alone and lost, and believed there was nothing for me anymore.

With $7 to my name, the only thing I knew was wrestling, so I decided to look for my dad. I managed to find my dad to train me, and I had my first try-out in 1996. The crowd did not like me at first, but I didn't care, and pushed through. Soon enough, I had a breakthrough and won 17 championships in the WWE. This success helped me to buy my parents a real home. I walked away from the wrestling career, as I believed I was done. I wanted to move to my next stage: films and the entertainment industry. In 2000, I was invited to host the SNL, and that's when Hollywood noticed me. At age 29, with no acting experience, I gave it all and worked hard to be where I am today. I received my Hollywood Walk of Fame star in 2017, which I am really proud of.

Dwayne's story tells us that when you come down to nothing, you use what is left. If you don't know where to start, you follow the footsteps of your idol. You only need 3 principles. You must believe, work hard, and never give up until you see the result: success.

Lionel Messi

Football is not only his passion but it also comes naturally to him. Encouraged by his grandmother to play with his cousin, despite being the smallest boy on the field, he joined the local club at age 4. Coached by his father, he would do nothing but practice, day in and day out. With his grandmother by his side, football was all he could dream of, and he grew a deep desire to become a professional. At age 10, his grandmother passed away, and this had a huge impact on Messi. He was so devastated that he decided not to play football anymore, and he quit going to the club. Luckily, his father managed to speak hope into him. Messi started to play again, with the intention to make his grandmother proud, and aimed to play the best he could.

By the age of 11, his parents noticed that he was still small (4'2) in height. Compared with other children of his age, he was small. After a visit to the doctor, Messi was told that he had a growth deficiency and, only after a special treatment, he would grow again. Disturbing enough, his family did not have the funding for the treatment. His dad worked hard and did everything to find the funds, but to no avail. He was left with no choice but to ask for financial support from the Newwell's Old Boys club. The club agreed to support, partially, until the Argentina economy collapsed. His father did not give up, and kept searching for finances to cover the treatment. With the same request, he asked the next football club, but they were not able to provide any support.

Not long after, Messi's family received what would become a lifetime offer, from FC Barcelona, in Spain. The club had noticed the 13-year-old boy's talent, and proposed a trial and medical expenses for his treatment, with the condition that he live in Spain. Although this sounded good, Messi and his family had to think about it, as it would mean that they would have to move to Spain. Looking at the conditions they were in, and with the dream of becoming a professional football player, it seemed a great opportunity, and so they moved. Within 2 minutes on the pitch, he was offered a contract, because he was very good. Coach Carles was so impressed with Messi's talent that he used the only paper he had–a napkin in his pocket– for both to sign. As promised, he received his medical treatment between the age of 13 and 14, and then he started to grow (today he is 5'7). During that time, he was on the field day and night, refining his gift, and each day, he would inject himself with growth hormones. He forced himself to train harder, and to be stronger, as his opponents were older, taller, and stronger.

With unpredictable moves, and driving by instinct, at 16, Messi won himself a spot with Barcelona's senior squad, and trained daily with Ronaldinho. At 17, and being the youngest player, he helped Barcelona win the UEFA Champions League for the first time in 6 years. He went to sign his first contract, as a senior team player with FC Barcelona, at age 18. Only 19, a top scorer and a world-class football player, Messi kept improving and breaking his own record. He received, at age 22, the prestigious FIFA World Player of the Year Award.

Let People Be Your Inspiration

Every score has always been a triumph to his grandmother. She was the first person who saw what we see today—Messi, top player, one of the best goal scorers in the world, and a winner of five Golden Balls, and three European Golden shoes.

"You can overcome anything if, and only if, you love something enough."
– Lionel Messi

Nick Vujicic
New York Times bestselling author, evangelist, and international motivational speaker for young and old

While growing up, Nick thought he would never be happy, as he did not understand why he was born without limbs. He struggled with depression and loneliness. It was not until a caretaker at school encouraged him to speak about his adversity publicly, that he found purpose in his life. Thanks to the caretaker, Nick turned his focus from himself, towards others, by speaking to small groups of students, at 17. Finally, by the age of 19, he began to understand the purpose of his circumstance, and decided to fulfill his dream. He started encouraging others with this, including sharing his life story. Today, he is the founder and president of an international nonprofit organization, Life Without Limbs, and the speaking company, Attitude is Altitude. Check out what he once said in an interview.

"People were looking at me; people were pointing their finger at me and laughing. I was born this way, and no doctor knows why I was born this way. Lady Gaga doesn't know why I was born this way. In my life, seeing everyone with arms and legs—my brother and sister have arms and legs—I never imagined that I would be happy; but we've got to understand that brokenness is brokenness, and hope is hope. Some people say, "Well, all you need is just to be positive." Well, it's easy for you to say—that's what I'm thinking. People who

have arms and legs, it's easy for you. I just want you to know, though, that I have come here to prepare a message for you, to let you know that there is hope beyond what you see. When, in life, we have things that come, and we try to figure out, well, who am I and what am I doing, and what's my purpose? Is there any purpose at all to my life in the end? I stand before you, without arms and legs, telling you right now that I am not disabled. There is something greater—something greater than the disabilities around you, or limitations around you. There is hope."
– N.Vujicic

One thing I really love about Nick's story is that it confirmed the ancient secret, which we touched on earlier, in Chapter 4, to be true. When you go through life, stressed, depressed, struggling, burdened financially, feeling lost, unhappy, unfulfilled, overwhelmed, and confused about your place on earth, things become complicated. Those circumstances stop you from seeing your true potential. The best thing you can do to help yourself move forward is to turn your focus towards others. You can see that if you choose to reach out to others, you will find your purpose. I share specific ideas, in Chapters 10 and 11, on how you can turn your focus from yourself. For now, I want to share Arnold Schwarzenegger's motivating story.

Arnold Schwarzenegger
Actor, author, politician, and businessman

Born in Austria, growing up with an abusive, alcoholic father, and living in poverty, Arnold was the youngest in the family. He and his older brother were forced to wake up every day at 6 a.m. Their father insisted that they do daily chores and schoolwork. They had to earn their breakfast with sit-ups, and it was mandatory for them to practice soccer every day, regardless what the weather was like. Arnold's father wanted him to become a professional soccer player. Though he trained vigorously, his heart was not in it but somewhere else. He believed he could do something different—anything more but soccer. Watching

Let People Be Your Inspiration

daily newsreels, he was getting more and inspired to change his circumstances. Stimulated by what he saw, he began to dream of a better future for himself. All he could imagine was to live in a happy place and become successful. With this new dream, he could not keep his excitement a secret, and he started to tell his schoolmates, "One day, soon, I am going to America." At 10, while reading a magazine, he came across a successful body builder named Reg Park. Reg, an actor with a business, an American empire, who had just won a Mr. Universe award, moved Arnold to take his first step. Reg became an inspiration, and Arnold believed he could become like his idol, so he made a decision and set himself a goal. "If Reg could do it, so can I. I have a plan: I'll become a bodybuilder, win Mr. Universe, go to America, make movies, then invest in business."

At 13, he knew what he wanted, and he started putting pictures of big and strong men on his wall, all over his room. He trained excessively every day and was not going to let anyone to talk him out of it, not even his dad. He joined the Austrian Army, at 18, to carry through his mandatory year of service. With an unshakable spirit, Arnold missed a couple of his trainings to participate in the Junior Mr. Europe contest, and won. Though he was sent to military prison for going AWOL, his triumph gave him more certainty not to give up on his dream. Soon after, Arnold won second place in another body-building contest, and was voted Best-Built Man of Europe. At 19, after his military service, he had then saved up money and took his first plane to London to participate in the Mr. Universe competition. Sadly, he did not win, but that did not stop him either, as by then, he was already in the spotlight.

"Failure is a necessary experience for growth in our own lives, for if we're never tested to our limits, how will we know how strong we really are? How will we ever grow?"
– A. Schwarzenegger

Exchange Setbacks for Winning

One of the judges was impressed by Arnold's physique, and offered to coach him for the next Mr. Universe competition. And yes, by age 20, he was the youngest to win the title—all his hard work had paid off. He was only 21 years old, and already a star in the bodybuilding world. The time arrived—his 10-year-old dream—and Arnold packed his bag, and off he went to the land of dreams, America, to make films. Shortly after, he graduated from the University of Wisconsin, with a major in International Marketing of Fitness and Business Administration.

He continued to win competitions and became the youngest winner of Mr. Olympia, at age 23, and until today, he still holds that record. Arnold was a millionaire by age 25. With a dream of becoming an actor, he did not have an easy beginning. He was denied on multiple occasions before getting his first role. Every casting director and agent would tell him, "Your accent is too strong. Your name is too long. Your body is too weird." But then his breakthrough came when Andy Warhol noticed his physique and used him as a model. Andy then later introduced Arnold to big names in the film industry. Arnold finally received his first role, in *Hercules,* in New York. His big moment was not until age 30, with a role in the hit movie, *Conan the Barbarian*. He received his action-hero roles, like *Commando*, *Total Recall,* and *The Terminator*, later on. It was all uphill from that moment; he became the Governor of California, in late 2003. Even though he had been a boy living in poverty, in a small village, today that boy is a movie star, businessman, and environmental activist.

"Be hungry for success, hungry to make your mark, hungry to be seen and to be heard and to have an effect. And as you move up and become successful, make sure also to be hungry for helping others." – A. Schwarzenegger

Let People Be Your Inspiration

Serena Williams
Tennis player

"I went on the courts with just a ball and a racket and a hope, and that's all I had."
– S. Williams

"I've had people look past me because of the color of my skin. I've had people overlook me because I was a woman. I had critics saying I would never win another Grand Slam, when I was only at number 7, and now, here I stand today, with 21 Grand Slam titles, and I'm still going. I have to tell each and every one of you that it doesn't matter how old you are or how young you are. You can achieve anything that you set your mind to, and I always say, 'If I can do it, anyone can do it.' The reason that I always say that is because I didn't grow up with things being handed to me. I had to work hard, I had to dedicate myself, and I had to be determined, and I was. It requires discipline, hard work, and determination. Most importantly, it requires self-belief because, like me, some people might not believe in you, but you have to believe in you."
– S. Williams

Investment Page

- Like Tyler, what would be your motivation to make money?
- Can you see yourself succeeding like all the others mentioned in this book?

Write your answers on the Investment Page.

Exchange Setbacks for Winning

With all these incredible true stories, I hope, by now, you're inspired. Let's not waste any more time; go to the next chapter to find out how you can discover and work on your dreams. I hope you're as excited as I am.

Let People Be Your Inspiration

Investment Page

CHAPTER 7

Invest With the Little You Have

"Where there is no vision, the people perish."
(Proverbs 29:18)

Where Do You Want to Go?

    To establish what you want in life, you must first know what you want. It sounds simple, but that's the honest truth. You need to know where you're heading. It is going to be very difficult if you don't know. Idealistically, your vision should help you to discover what you want in your life. Once you know where you are going, you make it easier for yourself to set effective and constructive goals. This should dictate your decisions and your choices. The awareness of your destiny will propel you to make the right choices. You know you are on the right path if your choices are lined up with your vision.

    It is important that you keep asking, "Am I heading in the right direction?" What you do every day must lead you to your end goal, which is your deepest desire: **What You Want**.

    I urge you to take time and invest in becoming familiar with your vision. Without knowing your vision, you will accept and settle for things you might regret in the future.

    For you to discover your ambitions, you must have clarity. Clarity will give you certainty, certainty will give you confidence, confidence will give you courage, and courage will overrule fear. When fear is diminished, action comes into existence, and through action, steps are taken forward to achieve greatness.

Faith Without Works is Dead

You and I both have an enemy that seems unbeatable, and it lies as well. It's called FEAR. Fear tells you that you will fail, so there is no need to try, no need to take steps forward, and no need to try anything new. Fear tells you that you can't trust the unknown, and that it is better to stay with familiarity. You know it already, and therefore it is much safer. If anything, this safety will hold you back from where you want to go or what you can become. Consequently, you keep pushing your vision away because it seems overwhelming, or you think it might never come true. Fear tells you not to start, or makes you question what others might think of your crazy idea. Please, read this sentence carefully: if you don't give it permission, fear cannot ever stop you from what you are meant to be or do. You and I have seen others using their potential to the max; they have learned to manage their fear by not giving it any authority. Please, do the same, and do what you are meant to be doing; don't let fear stop you. Fear will leave you behind whilst you are meant to be moving forward.

Why would someone read this book, or get similar encouragement from a different source, and still not change their life? Most likely, it would be *the fear of the unknown*. They are so afraid of failure that they will choose to stay where they are. Where they are is familiar ground, and that's what they know. I called it *the fear of the unknown* because you can't see the details of where you are meant to be going. So what! If things don't work out the first time, you then try it again, and again and again, until you see your positive result. *Failure is not that you have failed; failure is you building an experience that's making you becoming the master.* I hope you will not let *the fear of the unknown* stop you from doing what you would like to do. Don't let so-called *failure* be your end destination rather than your success. Keep going!

The will to face one's fear is to act.

Invest With the Little You Have

When you choose to keep going, you ignite your faith, and faith is the opposite of fear. Faith tells you to believe in what you have not seen yet with your physical eyes. You have confidence that whatever you are trying to achieve is already taking place and is accomplished. You look into the future with not only hope, but you are also filled with a strong sense of certainty.

Faith is only serving its purpose if it's put into action; it has no meaning if it's not followed with actions. Faith without works is dead! Hence, whatever you're believing in, your passion and dreams, you will have to put that into action by making a detailed action plan to see it all come to pass. Do you remember when I said that the fear of the unknown is without details? Yes? Well, I have something exciting to tell you. Before I continue, can I say I am glad that *the fear of the unknown* is without details? You might be thinking, "Cynthia, you are crazy. What do you mean?" Now, the exciting thing is...guess what? You get to design or create the details! You are in charge—the leader of your own life. You get to decide what and how, and for that reason you will get what YOU want, and not what someone else created for you.

Let me pause here and ask you, "How do you like your coffee or tea? If you don't drink either, then I want you to think of one of your favorite drinks. Let's say you like your coffee with milk and three sugars. You know exactly how you like your coffee. Now, imagine someone, who you don't know, coming up to you and saying, "I brought your coffee for you, just the way you like it." You take the coffee and realize that there is no milk in it, and you can't even taste the sugar—totally not what you want. You say to that person, "This is not how I like my coffee." The person then says, "This is what you asked me to get, so here it is, and I am not making you a new one." Your response is, "I didn't ask for this." As a final response from the person, they say, "Since you did not give me any detail on how you like your coffee, and you just said, 'Can you please bring me a coffee,' I thought you might like your coffee like mine, and so I gave you black coffee." The moral of this example is, *create and detail your own journey; otherwise, others might impose theirs on you.* It is your responsibility to discover what you want and to be creative with it. Don't worry; I am not going to leave you without giving you tools to design your *detailed action plan* and help you identify your gift. Let's find out how you can put your faith into action.

Allow your faith to help you create your own path.

Use What You've Got

In 2004, I moved to Australia for college. My first year went smoothly, and I had saved up money for the whole year. Already 5 months into the second year, I still had not found a job. I checked my savings account, and there was just enough money left for 2 months.

I didn't understand why this wasn't easy, but I chose not to panic, and kept searching. In the meantime, I was starting to feel bored. No job, no money—this was starting to frustrate me. The most annoying thing was that I was not able to go out or practice generosity. I enjoy being in the position of being able to say to a friend, "I'll get it for you," or "I'll pay," or to simply surprise someone with a small gift. So, now that I don't have money to do what I normally do, how then can I bless others? This led me to the next question, "How do I give without using any money?"

As far as I can remember, I have been living to give, and I realized that this attitude has become part of my identity. The situation I was in might not have seemed a problem to someone else, but for me, it was a different story. For months, I was thinking and trying to figure out what I could do.

At one point, I asked myself 2 questions: "Cynthia, what do you have? What do you enjoy doing the most?" "Well," I said to myself. "I like writing." Then, the coin dropped. "Cynthia, use what you've got, to give—your words on paper," I said out loud. I thought, then, that I could not only verbalize my encouragement to others but write it down as well, and give it to them. I was hesitant at first, because it would be my first time giving my words to acquaintances. Although writing, for me, had never been a mystery, I was not sure how people would take my scripts. I took courage and decided to take my own advice. The great feedback that I received encouraged me to take my writing really seriously. It was then that I made a solid decision and commitment: "Cynthia, no matter what, make sure you publish your words one day."

How do you find out the one thing you are great at? And how do you branch out from the one thing you enjoy? When people ask me these 2 questions, I often reply back to them with the *miracle* questions. "If anything was possible, and nothing was in your way, not even money, what would you like to do for work? How do you see yourself, and what work are you doing? Take a moment and see if you can answer those questions for yourself. Remember to write your answers on the Investment Page.

Here are three ways for you to inspire and single out your gift:

1. I want you to think as far back as you can, all the way back to your childhood. Do you remember the things you used to do and what you enjoyed? What made you happy when you were a child? What did you used to dream of?

You grow up with many dreams, visions, and wishes. Throughout the day, you imagine yourself doing so many things. You believe you can become anything you want, and create that idea you have in mind. As you grow older, the childhood imaginations and dreams start to fade away, one by one. It hovers on the surface of your heart. Sometimes you go back to your imagination and develop it secretly in your head. You design it all the way, from beginning till the end, but then you tell yourself that it is not possible.

Internally, you struggle to keep the dream alive, but with the pressure of the world, you unintentionally push it away, as deep and as far as you can. You keep living your busy life, yet that dream that you once tucked away pushes itself to the surface of your heart. You have this unsatisfied and discontented feeling, and don't know what to do with it.

If this is you, then it is time to embrace what you have always wanted to do.

Follow your childhood dream and make it happen.

2. You are simply good at what you do; it comes natural to you. From time to time, people, friends, and family tell you that you have a talent. You enjoy doing whatever it is, and it not only makes you happy but others as well. You have developed this unique skill to the point that it has now become second nature—as a matter of fact, you have mastered it. People close to you seem to point that out to you, yet you are uncertain if they are speaking the truth. Somehow you know they are right—it's just you—you seem to be the problem. Are you doubting yourself? Do you believe you don't have what it takes?

What is that feeling you have, when every time you think of taking the step, that feeling tells you not to take any responsibility? Is that feeling perhaps called fear? It keeps showing up, telling you that you can't do or become what you want to be come.

At the same time, you are aware of your talent, even if people around you have not encouraged you to pursue it. You know deep down that once you decide to give it your all, you will succeed. That feeling of *what would people say or think of me* is what is holding you back at this stage. Another time, fear spoke: "I have too many responsibilities to take care of. I have a family, and I still need to take care of this and that." This type of feeling will occupy and help you procrastinate. It will make you do everything but that one thing you wish to do. You hope to do it tomorrow, next week, next month, or next year, and while the days are flying by, you are still in the same position. Whether you believe what you know about yourself, or what people say about your talent, it comes down to you. Perhaps it is time for you to accept the encouraging words of your close ones. If they can see it, then that means it is in you. If it wasn't in you, they wouldn't have seen and pointed it out to you. What we see from the outside is a reflection of what's on the inside. Don't undermine your gift; take it seriously. If you enjoy doing something, take it further; release the pressure off yourself and do what you truly want to do. Do only what you love doing —anything else is a waste of time.

What others see in you—the outside is a reflection of what is in you. Do what you love doing, and make a career out of it, or take it to a higher level.

3. Who do you look up to (somebody you really like)? Let me rephrase it for you: who is your hero? What do you like about them? Do you aspire to be like them (obviously, in your own unique way)?

You might be walking around thinking, "I don't know what I can do. I don't know what kind of career would give me a sense of fulfillment."

I wonder who you had in mind. There is a reason why you chose those heroes or persons, and I am going to show you how they can help you discover your potential. Your heroes have qualities, values, and talents you like, and that is no coincidence. You like them because they say or do things you resemble and relate to. Whatever you see in your heroes is a reflection of what is inside you. It is like what I said in the previous paragraph, about what people close to you say and see in you. "The outside is a reflection of what's inside." In the same way, what you see in your heroes, which would be the outside, is a reflection of what is hidden in you—your potential. What you like seeing is what you admire; what you admire can be your inspiration; and what inspires you can lead you to your success.

As earlier mentioned, one of Dwayne's idols is Arnold. When he was uncertain about *the walk of success,* he decided to follow the footsteps of Arnold. See the table on the next page.

Arnold	Dwayne
Used what he had, his physique: Bodybuilding	Modeled Arnold and used his physique: Wrestling
Received his breakthrough in acting at age 30	Went into acting at age 29
Became Governor of California in 2003	Plans to run for president in 2020

Let those who you look up to be your inspiration.
Follow their path.

Your Personal Assets

When you think you have nothing to do or to give, the way forward is to look at what you've got. You were born with everything you need. Give attention to your personal assets—your intellect and body, your potential is in you. It's time for you to polish, grow, develop, and bring your uniqueness forward. No need to fear but to shine, for everyone to see, including yourself.

Your faculties are your greatest and most powerful personal assets you have. Let's look at them and examine what you've got, and how you possibly can use them.

Your Hands. Are you creative with your hands? You like to make and design objects. You like to cook or bake, or you are intrigued by how a surgeon can operate on the human body. You like to clean up things and make things look nice. You like to design, and the interior of homes is your thing. You like painting, as in art, or painting anything from houses to objects. You like to make sculptures, write, or play an instrument.

Whatever you find your hands on that makes and puts a smile on your face, that's what you need to develop. Use your hands to build, create, design, infuse with new life, examine, produce, fix, complete, heal, and make anything your heart tells you.

Your Mind. Are you a thinker? You like to solve problems and come up with great solutions. You like to provide advice and give others insight. You have a creative and innovative mind, and you know how to build and create new things that don't exist yet. You have a business mindset, and achieve to sustain others with employment. You like giving counsel to the authorities.

Your Voice. What can you do with your voice? Perhaps you like to sing, or you like to speak for those who don't have a voice. You act on behalf of those who are disadvantaged or have been done wrong by; you assist them with your voice and speak for them. You like to educate, explain, and get your thoughts across. You like to preach or make people laugh, and tell stories. You like to make decisions for others and bring justice.

Your Eyes. You like to capture moments of what you see, through photography and art. Others, and you as well, see you as a resource. You have materials and knowledge to offer, and others know that they can come to you for support. You like to create visual effects or develop new technology instruments. You like to record people live, or anything else you can get your hands on. You see what others don't see, and bring it to reality for all to see.

Your Heart. Some will say you have a humble or soft heart, but truly, you just like helping people. Your heart speaks of the injustice of the world, which makes you angry at times. You are quickly moved when you see others in a disadvantaged state. You have a great passion, and a compassionate heart, for children, youth, women or men, and animals. You stand up for equality, and like to take care of people from all walks of life. Nothing makes you happier than to see justice accomplishing its destiny.

Your Feet. You like to travel and discover new places, and share your travel experience. You like to take your feet to local places, and to countries where they need humanitarian support. You are fascinated by space, and see yourself traveling or working in that field. You like to travel for work or guide people around.

Your Body. You like the anatomy of people and animals. You like to take care of yourself. You like to educate on self-care and a healthy lifestyle. You like sport, and aspire to become a professional in the field. You like acting and dancing.

*Which *personal asset* do you see yourself most utilizing? Please write your thoughts on the Investment Page.

Don't look at what you don't have; focus on what you do have. What you already possess is what you are great at. I am sorry to break it to you, but nobody is capable of doing everything great, including you. You will make it easier on yourself by narrowing your ability down. Now, that doesn't mean you can't be creative and broaden your horizons. For instance, friends and family know that I can't sing, so I wouldn't spend loads of time and money to get a singing career. But what I possibly could do is write songs, as I enjoy writing, and that can never be taken away from me. Hence, you will always have one strong gift; that gift is developed in a talent, and that talent reflects your various skills. When your talents are multiplied and are in many areas of your life, you are fulfilling your potential. Once you start developing your major gift, you will see that all your other hidden minor gifts will start developing too.

Keep asking yourself, "Am I making choices that are leading me to where I want to go? Are my dreams, goals, and destiny being refined?" Dream big and challenge yourself; you will receive exactly what you ask for in life–nothing more, nothing less. If you want more, then ask for more by pursuing more. Don't limit yourself, and don't wait for anyone's permission. Avoid waiting for others, and don't let them hinder you from taking steps towards your dream. If you do, you will never arrive at your destiny. Find people who want to join and support you to reach your goal in life. Don't be surprised if you have to leave people behind. Some people would just try to pull you down and not contribute positively to your life. Make up your mind and decide not to listen to naysayers but to follow your heart, instinct, what you love doing, and above anything else, what you believe you can do. You only need one believer to become a winner in life, and that is YOU. As long as you believe, there is great hope for your future, and once you have hope, you are already rich—a winner in life. Whatever you hope to see or produce, don't let fear rob you, but take courage and JUST DO IT. If you don't do it, someone else will do it. It's either you make your own dream come true or you let someone else fulfill your dream, whilst looking at what you could have done or become.

Your Decisions

Two months before my surgery, I was thinking out loud: "I know I will make it. I know I will make it; I can't just die like that. There is so much I still want to do. I have not seen my biggest dream come to pass yet. I will have to make it. God is not done with me; the desires I hold are yet to be fulfilled. But what if..." I thought for a couple of seconds. Tears started to roll down my cheeks, and I cried. "What does this mean? If I don't make it, will this mean that ... No! I'll have to make it! I am going to ignore my fears and take courage. I will choose not to waste any more time but continue to help people finding their purpose and potential in life, like the way I found mine. When I survive the surgery, I will take this as a second chance to do life over again. *I will start with the beginning because I know the ending."*

I believed Europe and America had great opportunities regarding the process of publishing books. Plus, Australia had become a comfortable living zone, and there was nothing wrong with that. The problem is, like most people, when I am comfortable, I don't see much personal or professional progress. I am more motivated, purpose driven, and work better when I am uncomfortable. When things don't seem to be what I want or like, I get frustrated and angry at myself. The madness pushes me to change my situation and exchange it for something better. This would mean for me to move and change locations, to be closer to my dream. I recall having the best 7 days when I visited Ireland, in 2015. A country with many scenic spots, and extremely friendly people, with arms wide open to welcome any nation to their country—Ireland—that sounds right.

What would I do with all my stuff? I have a fully furnished, 3-bedroom apartment. I guess I could always store it, as it would be cheaper than paying rent for the whole apartment.

Decisions, decisions, decisions—if anything, we all have that in common. No one is excluded from making them. They come in all forms—exciting, fun, fearful, uncertain, good, poor, crazy, spontaneous—or no decisions at all.

Every decision you and I make, involve powerful emotions and solutions for our future. I have noticed that fear is the biggest emotion, which regularly stops us from what we want to achieve in life. No matter how you feel about a situation, you must do something about how you feel. Every decision leads to some form of consequence, whether it is positive or negative. At the end of the day, you and I are responsible for our own decisions. Some decisions will have long or short-term, small or big, impacts on our lives. It is important for you to make decisions and not prolong them. Take your time with the ones that need time. *The decisions you make today will determine your future; therefore, take them seriously.*

Ask yourself the following:

- Are these steps taking me where I want to go?
- Will this lead me to the goal or dream I have set my heart and mind on?

If your answers have been NO, then I hope you agree with me that you would have to alter your direction.

Our lifespan is limited, so why waste time if you can avoid it. To set proper priorities, be aware of your actions behind your motives. You can leave room for mistakes, but aim to do it better next time. Stay focused, and try not to lose sight of where you want to go; and while you are in the midst of your momentums, please avoid detours. The goal is to get to your destination with minimal detours. Enjoy and have fun with as much as life has to offer you, but take discipline and commitments—and your own words—seriously. Learn from you own experience, ponder on your own actions and behavior, and be determined to improve each time. Praise yourself for what you have done so far. Set the goal to improve yourself each year. You must have the attitude of, *I will do it anyway; I have nothing to lose but to gain!* Don't doubt the possibility!

Investment Page

Take time to think about where you are now and what you would like to achieve. You can start today by considering the following questions:

- Where do you want to go?
- What would you like to achieve this year?
- Are you aware of your passion, and do you know what your heart desires?
- What actions have you taken so far in achieving your dreams?
- Whatever you are doing at this stage of your life, are you still enjoying what you do?
- Are you heading in the right direction of your dream?
- Have you been detoured from your course? If yes, what happened? What was the hindrance?
- If you have been distracted from your course, have you gone back or designed a new course?
- Are you planning to give yourself the challenge, and make more effort to achieve more than last year?
- On a scale from one to ten, how satisfied are you with the course you are currently on? (ten being most satisfied)

Write your answers on the Investment Page.

Since we are all unique and have different wishes, I have put together a cool strategy for you. Chapter 8 will show you how to customize and refine your gift by using your 5 senses.

Investment Page

CHAPTER 8

Use Your 5 Senses to Get What You Want

You found the 5 senses tool kit! This tool kit is exclusive and is the only one you always will have with you. No matter where you are, you can always pull one or two out, and use it to your advantage. It is the best kit you will ever use, and it is simple to apply. But before we explore the kit, I need you to promise me to put your humor cap on. Are you ready?

Tool 1: Vision or Sight – The Eye

If you can see it, you can be it.

Your imagination is the most miraculous and powerful tool you have; it's with you 24/7. Sadly, at times, we tend to use our imagination for the wrong reasons, as setbacks can stop us from using our imagination the correct way. The challenges that come with setbacks can force you to imagine things you don't want to see, and this can be very discouraging. The purpose of your imagination is to take you to where you are meant to be: the future. Your imagination displays your dreams for you to see. The right imagination makes you feel the adrenalin in your body, and it gives you an invisible sense of fulfillment. With enthusiasm, it confirms your direction and tells you where you want to go. You were designed to imagine what you're capable of, what you are meant to be doing, and where you are meant to be living. It confirms your friends and family, who you share love with, and it helps you to see the full *you*—your potential. Your imagination is the blueprint of your life; it tells you what to do, when to act, and where to go.

I want you to believe and focus on the purpose of your imagination, as it is the greatest manifestation you have. Your imagination is first conceived in your mind. The birth of your imagination is what you see with your physical eyes. For instance, the clothes you are now wearing were once someone's imagination. Your imagination gives you the freedom and the authorization to bring the future into the present. Whatever you aspire to be, start today, by walking with the quality and the attitude of what you are imagining. The pictures you see in your mind are from your imagination. Exercise your imagination, every day, so you can keep it alive. Write it down; you can always refresh and give your mind a makeover. Use your imagination, and take your mental faculty to physical places. For example, if it is a dream house, go and check out that nice neighborhood, and allow your imagination to go wild. This will push you to make that extra effort, and to work a little harder, because you have seen it. It is your proof, and you saw it! *"If they have it, you can have it too."* It is possible, and you just need to believe it. Have pictures or models of what you want, in a place where you can see it, every day, and let that be your motivation.

One of the greatest gifts you received from birth is your imagination, so don't stop imagining or day dreaming—use it to the fullest. Your sensory factors will take you to where you are meant to be.

Your imagination is like Back to the Future.

Tool 2: Hearing or Sound – The Ear

Do you still have your humor cap on? I hope so, because you need it. I want you to pretend to be a spy. Yes, a spy! From today, I want you collect information from successful and interesting people you meet on your path. Be open to listening to what people have to say, and gain wisdom from it. You will meet people from all walks of life; some will give you useful advice and some will give you empty words. You can learn something from each person you meet. Those who speak with intelligence see it as free education, and eliminate interactions that are not relevant for their course. When you are networking with likeminded people, you listen more than you speak—listen and gain knowledge. Consider yourself fortunate when people choose to share their wisdom with you, as it is not compulsory for them to give you their time. It is only for your benefit, so don't take it for granted. At the end of the day, it might save you some time in your schedule, as they have already taken the time to study or research for you. Wherever you go, have an attitude and a mindset to gain profitable information. You can pass on that information to assist others; the more you have, the more you can give away. Be a walking resource for others so that when they cross paths with you, they find directions for their life.

Tool 3: Smell – The Nose

I have no doubt that you've already heard from the media or have read in an article that a dog's sense of smell has helped to save lives, or find predators or illegal drugs, or detect other objects. Dogs let their nose guide them; they use smell for directions, to detect danger, and to get what they want—food. While you have your humor cap on, this time, imagine that you are a dog. Don't laugh; I am going somewhere with this. Promise ;-).

In the same way, I want you to use your nose for guidance, and smell for directions. Sniff to see if the course you are currently on is the right path. Regularly, take the time to do a recap of what you want and where you want to be. Analyze and measure your time and effort you put into each goal. Keep asking the "Why" question: why are you doing what you do? What are your motives? Don't only ask the questions but also answer them. The best way is to write them down. If things don't smell nice, change or modify your direction. Compare your answers; are they still the same, and what could you change, if needed? Like the way a dog never stops smelling, you have to take on the same attitude. Keep questioning your own intention behind every behavior, choice, or decision. You are protecting your dream and your purpose in life when you keep smelling. Let your nose point you in the right direction. Be encouraged to know that while you keep sniffing around, you will eventually get what you want. If you have a dog, or know someone with a dog, you will know that dogs are always sniffing around to see if they can find anything to eat. As soon as nobody is watching, a dog will always take their chance to grab that food (whether the bin was open or a piece of cheese was on the table). Be on your guard and keep sniffing, because you never know—your opportunity might be just around the corner, and when it comes, grab it (regardless of what people say).

Tool 4: Taste – The Tongue

Did you know that you can't speak without your tongue? I am sure you did, but it's not something you think of every day. Your tongue is vital, and after the brain, it is the most authoritative organ you have. Your tongue gives your words power. Think of an authoritative person; when they speak, people obey or follow their words or instructions. When you make a promise to someone, your words become binding. The moment you speak, you activate your words.

Ask

This year, I told myself to ask for more things wherever I go. My friends and family know that I am not afraid to ask for things, especially if I think it is relevant and necessary. Although I have a reasonable attitude in asking for things, I still believe I could do better. I carried the concept of *"You already have the answer—'NO'—so you might as well ask, and position yourself in a 50% range to receive a 'YES'."* Without asking, you have a 100% margin of "NO." If you ask, and the answer happens to be "No," then you have not lost anything. However, if you receive a "Yes," you have not only gained but also have received something extra, because had you not asked, you wouldn't have that *extra thing*. For instance, you can ask for special offers wherever you go. Ask people for help; don't be afraid. Help comes in all sorts of forms, whether it is asking for advice, a hand to fix something, or a favor. It is in your power to ask, so ask for things, as it can save you time and money. Asking for things can speed up many processes that might take you a long time to achieve, and people love to help. Wherever you go, look for opportunities to ask for things, and you will be surprised at how much you can receive this year. You can simply change your life a little by asking for things.

Praise Yourself With Your Words

Have you ever considered that you are the first person who hears YOU when you speak? That's obvious, right? I am not being cheeky but am aiming to get a message across; in the meantime, feel free to laugh. Okay, since you are the first person who hears yourself, it is important to encourage yourself every day. Before you can believe anything, you will have to hear it first. You can read something, but it is not as powerful until it is spoken, or when you hear it out loud. When you start speaking motivational words to yourself every day, you will act according to what you are saying. The more you say it, the more you believe. Praise yourself, because no one will ever praise you as much. Your friends and family, and those who normally encourage you, are not with you 24/7, but YOU are. Say good things about yourself every day, and write it down if that is easier. After a while, this will become second nature to you. Say the things you believe and hope to achieve, out loud, with the intention of making your dream happen.

Taste

We use our tongue to taste, and although we all have different taste buds, it's good to ask someone to taste your food while cooking, or when it's finished. Even the best chefs will ask someone to taste what they are making, for a second opinion. Whatever you are working on, ask those who you can trust to taste it with you—ask for at least a second opinion. This is called being wise. There comes a time in your work where you will not see your mistakes anymore, and that's why it is important to have fresh eyes to go over what you are doing, and to make sure you have not lost your train of thought. Bouncing your ideas off someone who you trust will help and benefit you in the long run.

Tool 5: Your hands – Touch

Firstly, have you ever touched or felt what you're dreaming of? Let's say there is a type of car you hope to own one day soon. Why would you not go for a test drive and feel the buzz of the car. As I always say, "Have a taste of the future."

Secondly, your two hands can be of use at all times. Allow me to show you how.

Let's look at your right hand first: your right hand symbolizes your heroes, people you aspire to be, those who have gone before you and left a legacy, influencers, leaders, mentors, and coaches. Allow them to teach, educate, and pass on their knowledge to you. Make yourself available and seek opportunities to study them; learn from their mistakes and their triumphs. Get your hands on books, and read as many books that will help you gain insight and understanding. You have been given some clues from the past to use in the present. Let your right hand guide you so that the path you are on becomes lighter and easier. Good decisions are established through the right counsel and leaders. Be a step ahead of others, and allow your right hand to point you in the right direction.

Your left hand symbolizes your leadership: make yourself available to those who need your guidance. You and I are influencers; people should look at you and be inspired because of who you are. Build a character that can't be ignored, and be approachable for those who seek your advice.

I want you to look at both your hands, and allow your hands to create, design, and innovate whatever your heart desires. Don't limit yourself by not using what you've got, especially if you like to work with your hands. You are meant to find something that you are great at—manage it and give it your all. Everyone is called to lead in the area of their passion, but not everyone is called to lead people. Whatever you're meant to be doing is where you are meant to lead, with excellence. Use both your hands and lead what drives you.

"Once you discover what it will be, set out to do it and to do it well. Be a bush if you can't be a tree. If you can't be highway, just be a trail. If you can't be the sun, be a star, for it isn't by size that you win or fail; be the best of whatever you are."
– Martin Luther King Jr.

Investment Page

Here are 4 insightful questions that clients have found useful. This is to support you in approaching your setbacks differently from what you might have been doing.

- What is your imagination telling you?
- Where do you want to live? (Imagine or think about the country and your dream house.)
- What resources are you planning to use to reach your goals for the next 3 months?

Write your answers on the Investment Page.

I hope you are ready to increase the numbers in your bank account. The next chapter has insightful ideas on how to steer you in the right direction.

Exchange Setbacks for Winning

Investment Page

CHAPTER 9

Success Is Predictable

Would you believe me if I said that success is predictable? It is true! You can plan your success. You can create your dream life, simply by planning.

Have you ever been on a holiday before? I am just going to assume that you have. Now, did you or someone else have to organize the holiday in order to make it happen? Yes! Someone had to take the responsibility to make that holiday a reality. Let's say, you, or your friend, decided at that time not to take any action; would you have gone on that holiday?

Before we dive into the real story and explain the importance of the 5P's, I want to demonstrate the *predictable holiday* concept with you.

- Purpose of the holiday: pleasure, and you need a break from a busy lifestyle.
- Passion: you chose a place you are interested in; you are excited about your destination and can't stop talking or thinking about it. You're even counting the days.
- Planning: you make sure you book your flights and your accommodations, and plan to visit interesting places while you are there.
- People: you got in contact with authorities to get your visa or ticket; friends and family have given you the best advice for this trip; and last minute your best friend decided to come with you. You know it is going to be a great trip because he is coming. But

even if he was not, you would have made friends and enjoyed your holiday.
- Persistence: you were booking your flight online, and the payment did not go through. You tried again, and still it didn't work. You checked your account to see if there was enough money. You had enough money, and thought it must be the internet service. The next day, you tried again, and you received an error message to contact the airline company. You did not give up; you made sure you booked your ticket over the phone. And since you had already made up your mind, to not proceed with the booking was non-negotiable.

The secret to a prosperous life: to become successful, you will need your 5P's.

- Purpose
- Passion
- Planning
- People
- Persistence

If you want to live the life you really want, I would recommend for you to do everything with a **Purpose.**

You will have to ask yourself continuously, and analyze your reasons and motives behind your actions. Success will not just come your way; you will have to work for it. But hey, if you are working hard to achieve what you really want, working hard for your success is then not a chore but a pleasurable endurance. It is only the things you don't really want to do that become a chore. It feels like a chore because you don't have any passion for what's taking up your time. There is no love involved.

Passion always comes with a sense of love, and love gives you strength and hope. Love will guide you, and it will teach you patience to see the result of your desires. Love is kind, and will encourage you not to give up on your goals and dreams. Love is your biggest cheerleader in life, and no one can beat love, not even your closest friends and family. To be successful in life, you will have to plan it; and I hate to tell you, but that's the only way. You have to plan your success!

No one can **Plan** your success for you. Others can help, support, and guide you on your road to success, but not putting forth any effort will unfortunately lead you to an unhappy destination. *You must be prepared for your destiny.*

You will need **People** from all walks of life to get where you want to be. Your world, and the world together, becomes a team. The *world team* revolves for you and I, to give and to receive. I have given my friends, family, and community my positive and optimistic attitude, my quality time, and an ear to listen. I have expressed my love in many different ways, and I have shared my knowledge, including this book. Above all, you must care about people and their needs.

Until now, I have received way too much, and so have you. Allow me to explain. I am overly glad that throughout history, people never gave up on their dreams.

They **Persist**. They did not let anyone stop them from inventing or creating an idea but stayed focused. They kept going, developed themselves, confirmed their purpose in life, and thought of you and I. They were selfless and provided a solution for you and I to benefit from. They make our lives easier and more enjoyable to live.

- I thank the **Wright brothers** for the airplane; today, I can explore and visit other countries.
- I thank **Thomas Edison** for the light bulb; I don't have to sit in the dark (ha ha).
- I thank **Bill Gates** for Microsoft.
- I thank **Jeff Bezos** for creating a platform for me to publish my books.
- I thank **Steve Jobs** for the iPhone and the MacBook, as I possess them myself.
- I thank **Larry Page** and **Sergey Brin** for Google— an internet service I enjoy using.

- I thank **Walt Disney** for being one of the first to make outstanding animation movies, which I and children all over the world enjoy.
- I thank TV hosts for bringing information, laughter, and entertainment into my living room.
- I thank all authors for sharing their knowledge, ideas, and fantasies, by writing books to give back to the world.
- I thank cafes, bakeries, bars, and restaurants. If I want to treat myself, I just come to you and you serve me a nice drink or meal.
- I thank sports athletics for bringing me and my friends together when we watch a match or tournament. Thanks for the entertainment!
- I thank musicians, songwriters, and singers for allowing me to find therapy through their music, and to be entertained by them.
- I thank actors and actresses for expressing reality so I can relate and be entertained.
- I thank Pastors across the globe for bringing the word of God to me.
- I thank those who own and design clothes, household products, and creative objects.
- I thank the best doctors, lawyers, accountants, nurses, dancers, parents, chefs, humanitarian workers, and teachers, for giving their best to people.

I hope I am getting the point across; I can go on about everything I use or see around me. It was all once someone's idea, and they chose to develop their gifts and talents to the fullest. They persisted, never gave up, did not hold any potential back, and above all, they did not allow their setbacks to distract them from what they could do or become. I am thankful, as this is what I have received from all those people who never gave up their dream but persisted till the end.

I would like you to think of one of your favorite songs, books, electronic products, and furniture pieces in your house. Now, somebody created, wrote, or designed that item that has become your favorite. That means, whatever you thought of was someone's dream or vision, and the cool thing is that they made it happen. If that person gave up on their dream or vision, you wouldn't be enjoying that product today.

Your Mind

While the brain is the most powerful organ in the human body, your mind is the second dominant element or source you have. You are the only one who has access to your mind or intellect—no one else but you. Hereinafter, you are the only one who can change YOU.

I heard you want change. Did I hear right?

Ah, did you just say, "YES, I want change?"

Okay, let me tell you something profound and straightforward. In order for you to see change, to succeed and be a winner in life, you will have to renew your mind. *Change starts with your MIND*. You will have to change the way you think and how you perceive things. Your attitude results from your perception; your perception is derived from your thinking. Simply said, your attitude is the outcome of the way you think or feel about something. So, if you don't like the result of something, it is because of how you perceive it in the first place. You see things the way they are because of how or what you thought of. This also works the other way around; check out the formula:

your Thinking + your Perception = your Attitude
your Attitude = your Perception = your Thinking

To inspire, to impact, to lead, to contribute, to serve, to see positive results in your life, you must:

Start today by thinking positive.
Renew your mind, think differently, and create opportunities.
Change your mind and you will be a new person.

Know How to Manage Your Life

I strongly believe that the key to a prosperous life is to apply management principles to your life.

In order to live successfully, you will have to run your life as a business. In other words, you need to have your MANAGEMENT cap on. Let's think together; how is a successful business run?

- It's planned and structured, with expected positive results.
- It's organized.
- It's run with integrity and collaboration.
- It's measured throughout the year.
- It's always a couple of steps ahead of its competitors.
- It's run effectively to please its customers.
- It has its good and bad years, but it does not let the setbacks stop it from succeeding; it examines and learns from the core issues.
- It has the goal of always improving itself.

I hope you are starting to get the idea that you will have to adopt the same principles to manage your life. You can't slack off and take life just as it comes; you and I both know the results of poor management of companies. Eventually, they do not last in the market.

How does this apply to your life? Not only have you just found out how to run your life as a business, you also will have to change a few things in your days, weeks, months, and years. First, you will have to change your mindset; how you think will determine your decisions. Nothing can be changed if the mind does not accept the new idea. Once you make the decision to develop yourself, you will have to work on your habits. You might have the habit of procrastinating, not completing any task you started, or poor management skills.

To be successful, you will have to marry habits and discipline together—discipline will help you to get positive outcomes. It paves the way for you, yet requires diligence, honesty, and perseverance.

Habits

"How bad do you want it?" How bad do you want to make your dream a reality and achieve your goals? This is the part where I mean to teach about habits: how to adopt new skills, change old habits, and make you realize that what you have been doing for the past few weeks, months, or years has not been the best way to live if you want success. As a professional counsellor, specializing in Behavior Analysis, I speak from experience that modifying someone's behavior or habit could take a while, depending on the person's need. For me to support you, I would have to have a personal session or meeting with you. There are many self-help books out there that try to help readers to change their behavior or habits. For some, it works, by taking the author's recommendation, but for most people, they try it for a short time, and then they slowly slide back into their old habits. I am guilty and not excluded; I have also tried to change some habits in the past but have failed. What is it that makes us not succeed in keeping new learned habits? The best way for me to give you an understanding or teach you to modify your habits, is to give an example of my own life.

"I want to write many books and become a well-known author," I said to friends and family. This desire grew stronger every day. When I was not sleeping, I was dreaming of becoming an author. I would stay in libraries and book shops for hours, and get lost in some of the books. Every time I held a book in my hand, I saw a flash of my own book. I could not wait to see my name on a book cover. "What do I do with this passion?" One thing I knew for sure, and thought about millions of times in my head, is, "There is no way I will not publish books before I die; I must see it come to pass." I decided to let my vision guide me.

I started writing, and I changed the location in which I was living, to be inspired. I positioned myself with the right people, and met my publisher. Now, you need to know that I am not a morning person but have tried to change this habit. I still can't get up around 5 or 6am—that's just not me. I am a night person, and I have figured out that I actually only need to sleep 6 hours, and can stay up until late. For example, if I went to bed at 1am, I would then wake up at 7am, and I would be more productive. I avoid aiming to wake up at 5am and setting myself up for failure. I started using my time effectively. I allowed time to work for me instead of me chasing time. And every little bit of time I got my hands on, I spent it on writing this book. I stopped going out as much with friends, and told friends and family that I was working on an important project. To me, this is what I wanted, and I could not relax but worked hard to finish this adventure I started. You see, no one—and I mean no one—told me to change my habits, to work hard, or to plan my time differently.

Today, I realize that habits can only be changed based on your vision, dreams, and your willpower. It really comes down to, "How bad do you want it?" And you will have to renew your mindset if you want it! Renew your mind with positive inputs.

Your vision will dictate everything. Having a vision helps you to make the right decisions, and the right decisions lead to effective and positive habits. Positive habits are the evidence of progress, and progress means results. Results reflect your achievements, and your achievements are a mirror of your success.

If your dream is so important, and you know exactly what you want, then you will do anything to make it happen. Trust me, this is true, and I am talking from experience. I am also 100% sure that those who have made their dreams come through would agree with me on this. Once you are sure of what you want, you will choose to discipline yourself, and this will come naturally to you. Discipline is a behavior that demands and imposes positive pressure on you to reach your goals. Precisely, discipline is the actual force behind your self-control. Without discipline, it is almost impossible to see your vision come to pass.

You will have this sense of drive, and can't help but see your dream fulfilled. Yet again, a vision is a passion you cannot let go. Dreams or visions stem from a serious passion that you can't let go of, and any excuse you can find to spend time on it, you will take it. No one will have to tell you what to do; you will find ways yourself to accomplish the idea that is in your head.

Vision comes before discipline and habits.

Planning

*When it's on paper, it is clear,
and it makes more sense when you see it.*

When clients ask me to assist them with planning their goals, I first challenge them with the following notion: "Planning is a combination of time and change." Time and change are interchangeable and feed on each other. You can't have time without change, or change without time. As time is always moving forward, and does not travel back, so is change moving and is inevitable. You and I can't stop time or prevent change from happening in our lives. This seems to be out of our control; there is nothing we can do about it, other than to accept time and change. We live in time and change. It is the frame of our lives, and within that frame, you and I are given the possibility to influence our lives.

Change comes with choices. Imagine someone asking you to choose a flavored ice-cream; they give you the power to control the flavor. The moment you take the choice away, you take control away too. Throughout our lives, we have choices, even though, at times, it might feel as if you don't have a choice. But that's not really true; you always have a choice to do what you want. Change tells us that nothing will remain the same and, therefore, some changes we can make ourselves. There are some changes that you and I are in control of. Think of it this way: if you don't like where you live, you can move from your location. If you are not happy with your current skills, you can educate yourself with self-development materials or any other course. Because change comes with choices, you have the ability to plan ahead. Using the same example, you can plan your new location or plan your next available training. Though change seems beyond our control at times, there are things in our lives we frequently have control of. We should never use change as an excuse, saying we can't manage, but plan our goals and dreams accordingly.

You control time by planning. What you do with your time totally depends on you. How you manage, or use or invest your time, stems from where you are heading in life. You will only divide your time accordingly if you have a clear picture of where you're going. If not, someone else will plan your life for you. Time can only benefit you when you use it properly. Whatever you invest or put your time in is what you will receive.

To be in control is to make choices for yourself.

Finally, we have come to the details of planning. It might sound obvious, but the best way to plan everything is to record everything. Hopefully, you have the *Follow Your Dreams Inspirational notebook* to write all your goals and dreams.

Start today with writing down your dreams, visions, and goals. Every time you think of something, record it. This will help you to stay focused.

One particular client came to me with many questions on how to start her new business idea. Though she believed in her impeccable idea, her biggest concern was her finances. She was extremely worried about all the tasks and costs involved, and almost perceived her business dream to be impossible.

Her first mistake was that she was literally thinking about everything at once, and asking the wrong questions to begin with.

Your first question should never involve the cost. Rather, write your plans down first, and break your ideas down. Write what you see, and how you see yourself in the future, and then you ask the following:

- "What do I need to do to get there?"
- "Who can I talk to or seek advice from?"
- "What resources can help me to develop this idea?"

Then you ask, "How can I get the funding? What can I do in the meantime to collect the starting funds, if I can't get a loan from the bank? Do I need to create or produce something small first, or sell what I don't need, to get me where I truly want to be?" By the way, keep trying with different banks for loans; sooner or later, there's going to be a bank that will believe in your vision.

Once your passion and desires are on paper, you will get a better perspective, and you will feel much more relaxed. Understand that all the information was trapped in your head, and now you have made room for you to think bigger and be more creative.

Second, plan your success by setting time apart, and give your goals dates; this is very important. You need a large amount of time to think about how to get to your goal, and to achieve your set dates. Be realistic in your approach, and schedule time every day to do your research or work. Use your 5 senses to get what you want. Let no day pass by that you are not working on your dream. Always do what you can, and watch how your life unfolds.

"Success is no accident. It is hard work, perseverance, learning, studying, sacrifice, and most of all, love of what you are doing or learning to do."

– Pele

You can only invest in others when you invest in yourself first.

The Keys to Becoming Financially Successful

"The greatest reward in becoming a millionaire is not the amount of money that you earn. It is the kind of person that you have to become to become a millionaire."

– Jim Rohn

You may be like me, and have wondered what made some people financially successful, and others not. "What were they doing differently from the rest of us?" I decided to find out myself and, whilst studying what successful people do, I came across some interesting facts. I had noticed common patterns, but I still did not understand until I came across Dr. Munroe's teaching on financial success. I was blown away on how he made me see the obvious. I had heard people saying that you just have to find something to do, and then the money will just come. But I knew that wasn't it; I knew there was a secret or a great principle behind people's financial success, because not everyone is able to manage their finances well. We all have heard of people who had become millionaires and lost it all. Or some people who have a good business but are still working very hard and are in debt. Yet there are people like Bill Gates, the McDonald (brothers Richard and Maurice) family, and Oprah Winfrey, who are truly financially successful.

Dr. Munroe teaches 4 key principles or stages that people like Bill Gates follow unintentionally. These are Production, Multiplication, Distribution, and Domination.

You will have to produce a product or come up with a good idea that involves a need, which can be shared with others. To encourage you, you only need to come up with one idea first and manage it well, like Coca-Cola (founder, John Pemberton), which only produced drinks.

Whatever you come up with needs to be put in a system for multiplication. It might sound silly, but you will have to make more of it—so much that you will have to distribute to different places and countries. Down the track, your reproduction can be slightly different from the original. For an example, at first, Coca-Cola produced the original flavor with a red label on the bottle. Today, there is also vanilla and stevia flavors, which are labeled with cream and green colors. Second, you must stay productive and manage it too; your success will end when you stop reproducing.

You must always dream big! Don't limit yourself and distribute your product only in the city where you started; you must take it further and distribute it to the rest of the world.

Last point, it's very important to know who you are and that what you produce is the best on the market. What you produce must be different and unique. That is the only way you will stand out in the market.

So, there are 6 strategies you need to remember in order to see exceptional results for your finances:

1. Change your mindset to be going in the right direction to achieve your dream.
2. Produce an idea—one good idea that you are great at—and be creative.
3. Your idea is a solution to a problem or need.
4. Multiply the product—reproduce what you produced.
5. Distribute to everywhere you possibly can think of—share it with the world.
6. Influence; be the greatest in what you do, and you will be unbeatable.

You only need one idea!
You are not born to do everything but only to do the one thing you are great at.

I Saved the Best for Last—Your Creativity

Find a solution first, and money will follow you.

You must learn to be creative; the lack of creativity to produce is a dead-end to success. You will have to expand on that dream, vision, or idea of yours.

To only imagine will not lead you anywhere. If you are not a creative person, let your surroundings or environment inspire you. Pay attention to the need in the world; notice the creativity in everything—hold, touch, feel, and experience the mystery behind the things you see. After a couple of years of studying successful people, I found the real secret to their financial success—and it is not luck. The key to increasing the numbers in your bank account is for you to create an idea that will solve a problem or bring a solution to a need in the world. You do this by starting small, or with the little you have, and build what you created first, to get the big thing. **Mark Zuckerberg** and **Elon Musk** are only two examples of many. Mark created a platform for socialization, and Elon first invented PayPal, a simple and safe way for online payments.

Here are the steps for you to have money following you:

- Find a solution to the challenges of humanity.
- Recognize or discover the problem or need first.
- Think of an idea of how it can be solved.
- Don't limit your sense of creativity while you are thinking on how to solve the issue.
- Connect with the right people who can help you make it happen.

They use their passion to solve a problem.
They became rich, and as a result, they live in abundance.

One Good Reason to Pursue Financial Freedom

Imagine planning a surprise birthday party for a friend. Your budget is $60 because that's all you can afford. I want you to start thinking about what you need to make it a great surprise party. I am sure, by now, you think, "$60—that's not much at all!" You are probably right! Nevertheless, you managed the money and still came up with a surprise party. Okay, let's say you don't have a budget, and have been financially independent for the last 5 years. Would you agree with me that you will invest more in the party? Yes, you would. The pursuit of financial freedom is vital and will give you great access to do more for others and yourself. You will be able to give more back to the world. To give you two examples, Tony Robbins, with the organization, Feeding America, aims to stop hunger for those in desperate need in the USA, and feed a billion, in six and a half years—2024.

Had he not been wealthy, he wouldn't be in that position to feed those children—and don't forget, he started off with nothing. His dedication to feed the hungry stems from a time, at the age of 11, when someone gave him and his family a free meal on Thanksgiving. Today, his actions and attitude towards financial freedom has caused him to serve others.

Bill & Melinda Gates Foundation announced, in April 2018, that they will pay $76 million of Nigeria's debt. Japan had loaned this money to Nigeria, in 2014, to help Nigeria eliminate polio. Had Mr. Gates not followed his passion, he would not have been in a position to help.

I hope I have awakened any hidden cause that you're passionate about, and that you will not take this moment in your life lightly. I hope you will follow your heart and make a difference in the lives of those who are in need.

You can only help others when you invest in yourself first.

> **Investment Page**
>
> Here are 4 insightful questions that clients have found useful. This is to support you in approaching your setbacks differently from what you might have been doing.
>
> - How have you been using your time?
> - Do you see the need of becoming financially independent?
> - If yes, what did you have in mind? What are your plans to succeed?
> - What would you like to offer the world?
>
>   Write your answers on the Investment Page.

So far, we have covered some of the most important aspects of becoming successful. Hopefully, by now, you understand that success starts with the mind, and you will have to apply management strategies for your life. Your view and how you think, what you believe and your future outlook, plays a huge role. I hope, by now, you are beginning to know what you want, and have an idea of how to shift some few things around to get closer to your goals. Don't forget that learning principles are not enough; you will have to put them into practice to achieve what you really want.

The next chapter will give you a clear picture of *The Ancient Secret*: switching your focus, looking beyond yourself, and discovering your true potential through the act of kindness and service. You will not be disappointed by life if you follow this strategy. Let's check it out!

Investment Page

CHAPTER 10

Living Is Giving

The greatest reward you can give yourself is to invest in others.

    Friends and family ask me how I stay so positive and optimistic, and what the secret is to the contagious smile on my face during every season. I then tell them to love life by believing that in the end, when you manage your life well, everything will work out for you. I tell them not to take anything for granted, and to carry an attitude of appreciation, gratitude, and humbleness towards others.

    I was lucky to have both my grandmother and Rebecca to teach me to consider others around me. Wherever you go, try and acknowledge people, as every person you meet is as significant as yourself. You don't know what you can mean to a person; your encounter could be their hope or strength for that day. Do not underestimate what you can mean for another person. We can all play our part and be someone's miracle. Since we are all born with a purpose, and we are not here by mistake, people who you cross paths with are not a coincidence. Over the years, I have been fortunate to share with others my love, gifts, finances, and time. Thanks to my upbringing, I have been aware of the secret of *switching your focus*, and always have found pleasure in doing so. The interesting factor about this life secret is that once you share what you have, you receive more in return. It might not be the same or exactly how you expected it to be, but you are always rewarded more.

    What you're about to read in this chapter are practical ways or suggestions on how you can *Turn Your Focus*, or rather, exchange your setbacks for winning. I share examples of the people in my life, and how they turned their focus towards me while they were going through their own setbacks.

A Year's Supply

I was sitting in class, thinking how I was going to pay my rent and food. I saved enough money for the first year of college. It had already been 2 months into the second year, and I still had not found a job. John, sitting next to me, said, "Ruth, my wife, and I were thinking of paying for your groceries." As I was looking at John, I could not believe what I was hearing. I had never heard something like that before.
"What did you just say?"
"Well," John said, "We want to support you a little because we know that being a college student is not always easy, especially when you are overseas." I had no words at first. With a soft voice and a confused mind, I said, "Thank you; it is as if God spoke to you." The thing is, I had never mentioned anything about how short of money I was. John and Ruth had no insight about my circumstance. They just decided to show an act of service and kindness to me. When John took me to the shops, while I was standing in the aisle, I was so overwhelmed and could not even grab what I needed. He was so kind, and told me to get everything I needed. "Everything?" I asked.
"Yes, everything," he replied, and he started to place food in the shopping cart, items I normally don't even consume. I thought that was funny, as I normally would not have picked them out. The miracle did not stop that day. Could you believe that John and Ruth happened to pay my groceries for the rest of the year? Yes, they did.

True Generosity

Lissa and Tod are the most generous couple you could ever meet. I mean, this couple has taken generosity and the act of kindness and service overboard. They go beyond themselves, and I am always inspired when I am around them. Lissa and Tod have shown and taught me real generosity through their lifestyle and who they are.

They are living proof of the meaning of generosity. From the moment I met them, they embraced me into their family and treated me like their own. They include me in their family activities, and I have always felt the genuineness and warmhearted intentions behind their act. Every birthday, Lissa took me out shopping, and will also take me out for dinner, together with the family. During the shopping, she makes sure I had the VIP treatment, and insisted that I get whatever I wanted, with no budget attached. Lissa is the type of person, when you give her a compliment about any of her accessories, or anything in her house, she would then say to you, "Have it, you can take it; it's yours now." She means it and truly wants you to have it. She does not hold onto anything but loves to share all she has.

And if she knows that you like something, she will then go and buy it, and surprise you with it. She is a great listener and has *radar* to catch anything, with the intention to make a difference in someone's life. There has not been a time when I was in her presence that she did not send me home with extra food and groceries. With a positive attitude, Lissa does not fail to encourage those around her. When I am around her, I am constantly reminded to see the best in everyone.

Sharing Tears

I remember that day, the day that I wanted to cry, and I wanted to let it all out. A family member had passed away. I was close to her and had known her almost all my life. She was a special woman; we had differences, but I loved her for who she was. Standing in church, Primrose grabbed my hand, and I was pleased that it was her standing next to me. I don't know anyone as kind as Primrose; she is lovely, transparent, and very warm at heart. Before I knew it, she was crying, and her tears seemed unstoppable. She cried so deeply that all I could say was, "Thank you."

"It's okay, Cynthia," she repeatedly said. What was going through my head was, "Thank you for crying for me; thank you for doing this for me. Because I couldn't do it, you did it for me." To me, she was saying, *I got you, Cynthia*. It was as if she understood me. I was so moved beyond understanding, and overwhelmed with the love she showed, shedding her tears for me. No one has ever done that for me. Primrose was generous with her tears. While mine were held up, she gave me hers. As I clung to her, it felt as if her tears were mine, with no words to describe it, other than to say that I was crying, and my tears were on her cheeks. That day, I experienced something new. Primrose's tears showed me that kindness is not only an outside act, but it can also come from within—an act of kindness that most people wouldn't think of, and one which the majority are not familiar with.

*Can you guess who the special woman was? Keep reading; you'll find out soon.

The Letter Box

One day, during my college years, I went to check the letter box and found a white envelope with my name on the front. I turned the envelope to see who it was from, but there was no name on the back. I opened the envelope and, to my greatest surprise, I found $500. I can't remember what I felt, but all I know is that I was very much moved by this anonymous gift. Five hundred dollars, at that time, was a lot, and it meant the world to me. Until today, I still don't know who left me the white envelope with the money. Whoever it was, I take this opportunity to thank you.

Hands and Feet

Akua, a woman with a heart of gold, doesn't keep the gold to herself but shares it with whoever comes on her path. She allows you to take your pick, and will not stop you if you need more. While in recovery from my major surgery, in 2016, I was blessed to have Akua in my life.

When I was not able to walk, she helped me walk. She fed me when I could not eat by myself. When I could not stand, she supported me. When I could not shower or clothe myself, she took over. When I needed someone to tell me that everything was going to be alright, Akua said those words. How can one give all her love and care for another person? When you feel like you are at your lowest point—vulnerable and dependent—someone offers to stretch out their hands to you. How can you understand that? She did not only use her words but confirmed her promise with her hands and feet. You can't understand that! The only explanation is to say, "It's called the act of service and kindness—generosity."

So, where did this all come from? It all starts with you. When you start to show others kindness, and go out of your way to serve and think of others more, you will be rewarded with greatness. Your life will be filled with richness, and no matter what you might go through, you will always get your strength back—because the right people will keep you going. While you take your mind off yourself, you automatically push yourself forward. *Helping others and expecting nothing in return is an imprint you can leave on someone.*

* To see a full-sized, colored picture of Lissa, Primrose, and Akua, please go to www.ExchangeAndWinLife.com.

7 Ways to Show Kindness

Living your busy life, you might wonder how you can make a difference in someone's life. As time consuming as it sounds, making a difference in someone's life does not have to take up all your time. Let me encourage you: "You do not need to go out of your way to show your act of service or kindness." It is very simple; all you need to do is make yourself available, and you will start seeing the need around you. When you open up, you will notice things you never did before. You can do it on the go! Here are 7 fun and simple ways.

1. Be on the Lookout

Not long ago, I was on the bus, going to work, and a young lady got on the bus. She swiped her card to pay her fare, but for some reason, her card was not working. The bus driver probably must have gotten out of bed on the wrong side, as he was grumpy, unfriendly and not helpful. He started arguing with the lady, and she burst into tears and was told to get off the bus. While no one had pressed the stop button, the bus driver pulled over and stopped the bus. I was sitting far back, and heard the argument, and the lady's cry, caught my attention. I immediately jumped out of my seat, walked up to the front, and said to the bus driver, "I'll pay her fare," and put my card on the payment machine. I believed she was able to reach her destiny on time, and I was honored to have made a difference in someone's life, with only 2.15 euros. I have to be honest with you, I was disappointed that I was the only one who got up to pay this lady's fare. Other than myself, no one attempted to help this lady out; all were sitting and watching what was happening. When I got off the bus, I was actually sad, and thought, "At least 2 or 3 people should have gotten up and attempted to pay for this lady's fare." I wish that would have been the case. The others on the bus were mainly focused on themselves, and were unavailable or not on the lookout to help, but I was.

2. Doing Something Extra

Sevda has a great passion for food, and you probably could say she is a food guru. If you would ask her to name one favorite thing to do, on any day, she would say, "I like baking, and it is so simple; you just throw everything in the mixing bowl, and then put it in the oven." When I think of baking, I am thinking of the effort I first need to put in to get all the ingredients, and then to measure everything. Pfff, if anything, that sounds like too much work for me, plus I don't like measuring things. The great thing is that Sevda finds pleasure in baking, and she loves it. The first thing Sevda thinks of, when she receives an invite to an occasion, is, "What shall I bake? I want to bring a cake." Sometimes she will use an old recipe of her own, and other times, she will use the traditional cookbook. No one ask Sevda to bake a cake and bring one, but she chooses to share her gift with those

Living Is Giving

around her. Since Sevda was already invited, she doesn't see it as a problem to do something extra while being in the company of others. This is one of her ways to show her kindness.

3. Paying for Lunch for a Stranger

Jessica K. clocked out. "Finally, work is finished. I will have to stop at the shops and get some food for tonight," she thought. Just before the entrance of the supermarket, she quickly acknowledged a young lady coming up beside her. She wore a blue coat and black pants, and had chocolate-colored skin and black hair. "Hi, how are?" Jess said.

"Hello," she replied.

"How has your day been?" Jessica asked.

"I am good, thanks for asking. I am actually glad you said hi to me. I am a student here and have been living here for a month. I have not made many friends yet and don't know anyone, really."

"The pleasure is all mine. I am in a little bit of a rush, but if you don't mind, how about I take your number? I'll give you a call sometime this week; I will take you out for lunch, and it's on me," Jessica said.

"You would do that for me?" the young lady asked.

"Yes! And why not do something nice for another person?" Jessica replied.

4. At The Workplace

Another busy day at the ward, short of staff, and Caitlin just went home sick. This is the third time this week that I have to do overtime. "Emily, could you please give me a hand with the next patient, and please get the instruments ready for the surgery," Nathan said.

"Of course, I will get on it." Things had not been easy for Nathan lately; his wife had undergone surgery. And with the overtime, Nathan had been traveling back and forth between the hospital he worked in and the one his wife was admitted to last week. I had noticed that Nathan was only eating crackers—no decent sandwich or meal—and today is Friday. With wrinkles around his tired eyes, I wondered when the last time was that he had enough sleep. I was glad we were working on the last patient, and then we could go home and rest.

I couldn't stop thinking about Nathan when I got home, and decided to call my mother. "Mom, you need to come over; I need your help to make lasagna for a colleague of mine." "Okay, I'll be right there. Give me 20 minutes; I will stop at the shops to get a few extra things," mom said.

Nathan should be in today; he has been rostered to start at noon. "Hi Emily, how are you?" Nathan said, while walking in the door.

"I am great! Just a second, I need to grab something for you. Nathan, I have seen you doing the overtime, and I know your wife is in the hospital. You have been visiting her back and forth, and I assumed you wouldn't have the time to cook yourself a nice meal. Please take this as an act of kindness. I made lasagna for you, and I know this is a difficult season for you."

"Emily, you shouldn't have," Nathan said, with a wobbly voice and teary eyes. He was trying hard not to cry, but then his tears started to drop. The more he was trying to stop his tears, the more the tears were coming. "I am so sorry, Emily, that I am crying. It is just that no one has ever done something like this for me before. I appreciate you, and yes, I do love lasagna."

"Great! Enjoy it," I said with a smile.

* To see a full-sized, colored picture of Emily, Jessica K., and Sevda, please go to www.ExchangeAndWinLife.com.

5. Be on the Lookout When You Are at the Shops and at Restaurants

An easy, time effective way of showing kindness is to become aware of the people who are serving you at the shops and at restaurants. You can easily show an act of kindness by acknowledging them and appreciating their service to you. Give them a simple smile. Please don't look at them, thinking, 'It's your job; you're getting paid to serve me, so you have to do it anyway." No, this is not the right mentality or attitude. You don't know what that person behind the till, or the waitress, is going through. You don't know their past struggles or how far they have come to serve you. You have the power and the influence to make a difference in their life by simply saying hello, addressing their name, and sincerely asking how they are. Choose to be that person that wants to make a change in someone's life.

When you go out for dinner, or are sitting at a coffee shop, since you're already there, take the time, look around, and see if you can spot someone who you can bless. The person doesn't need to know anything; all you need to do is take their table number, and while you pay your bill, you pay theirs as well. I want you to think for a moment what impact you will leave on this person's or family's life. They will go and tell their friends and family what you did. If that happened to you, wouldn't you tell your friends and family? I would.

6. The Homeless

There have been times when I walked past the homeless and turned a blind eye, with a sense of guilt, and other times where I could not wait to give them my attention. I am not a fan of giving money to a homeless person, but I enjoy giving food. I guess I don't like giving them money because of the fear that I might contribute to perhaps their addiction. I have learned, over the years, not to let that mindset stop me from giving my support to those who are less fortunate. Here is a way...

Look in your fridge and give some of your food away. Most people buy way too much when they do groceries. They stock too much food in the fridge and, eventually, some of the food goes bad. Don't waste food; don't wait until it goes bad and you have to throw it away—give it away before then.

Let's say you have a special route that you take daily, whether it is a street or area, where you know homeless people stay—you can prepare and take them something. Perhaps cook some extra food; take it with you, and on your way to work, you can give it to them. Or, let's say, you passed that bridge where you often see a homeless person—give them some of your leftovers. You get the idea.

What I occasionally do, when I go for dinner, which is often in the city, I order extra food, and on the way home, I give that extra food to a homeless person.

Could you believe, on numerous occasions, when I was looking for a homeless person to give that extra food to, I couldn't find one? It seemed as if all the homeless people had suddenly disappeared. I honestly had to look for one by going at least twice around the block, lol. Then it dawned on me that I picked the wrong days. Those days were the rainy days, where they were all hiding from the rain; they sheltered themselves to keep dry. Hence, false alarm; the homeless people are still on our streets, and we all still have work to do.

7. Friends and Family

You can show your kindness to your friends and family by active listening. Generally, people tend to express their thoughts and feelings by speech, from their experiences or stories. You will be surprised what you will discover when you pay a little attention to people when they speak. They will give you clues, and it is up to you to turn those clues into acts of service, and make a difference in their lives.

You might know a family who is struggling, or families who are perfectly fine. Either way, it is always nice to give a hand when people are not expecting it. And sometimes what may seem great might not be the case. You can look at your neighbors and not know that they could use your help. It's considered normal for them not to ask for your help, and this could be because of their upbringing. Despite what we know, imagine if you stretched out your hand, and how that could impact their lives. You might think, "I don't have the time," and you're right; neither do I, but that doesn't mean we can't make changes in each other's lives.

What I always say to clients is, "You do it as you go!"

- As a family, you can support someone or another family who is less fortunate.
- Take a child, from another family, with you when you go as a family to do activities.
- You might know someone or a family with disability needs; find out what help they might need.
- Single parents can take turns to pick up their children from home and school. There is no harm in asking what a family or a single parent might need.

You and I can always stretch out our hands and give someone a break, allow them to breathe, and gather their thoughts. This is so that they can find strength again and get back on their feet. You and I can't help everyone, but we can make a difference in one person's or a family's life. We can always help change a person's or a family's life. Be a family's or a person's hope, and help them exchange their setbacks for winning.

Hopefully, you understand that making a difference in someone's life is complimentary to you. See it in this way: you are the one that gets to impact this person's life, and they will remember you for as long as they live. I don't know about you, but I think that's pretty awesome. Like some of the stories I shared earlier, those friends of mine had no idea what impact they had on me until they read this book. My question to you is, "Whose life are you going to change, and how many people will you leave your imprint on?"

You can never regret making a difference in someone's life.

> **Investment Page**
>
> Any ideas on how you can make a difference in the lives of the people you share your life with?
>
> Give yourself a challenge, and think of how you can help someone exchange their setbacks for winning (a person or a group of people you're not close to).
>
> Write your answers on the Investment Page.

Now that you have knowledge in the various way of impacting those around you, lets extend ourselves and take it globally, in the next chapter.

Investment Page

CHAPTER 11

Share Your Investment

Your Best Today and Tomorrow

Would you agree that it is normal or almost expected from you to show your appreciation when you receive a gift from a friend? And would you also say it would be rude for you not to say thank you; especially if it were a gift that you did not expect, or one that means a lot to you and is a valuable gift that you know you will hold on to as long as you live. With that thought in mind, you and I were given the earth as a gift; none of us had to work for it but were all given it.

So far, we have been looking at ways to share our investment, or rather to give back a part of ourselves. Another way of turning your focus, or to give, is to take care of our planet; by doing so, you show your appreciation. How you perceive the earth comes down to your attitude. We must learn to manage what we have. It will not only help us today but also help those who are coming after us. We do this by looking beyond ourselves and keeping the next generation in mind. We are responsible for the earth, and if we don't take care of it, we will lose it all one day.

My intention is not only to bring an awareness and to promote the protection of our environment, but also to teach you another way of how you can apply the *exchange setbacks for winning* principle, to help you move to the next phase of your life.

Exchange Setbacks for Winning

Simple things you can do to help the environment:

- Educate yourself and others.
- Try to take your bike or walk to places.
- Volunteer or join your local global organizations.
- Don't waste water or litter; plant a tree in your yard.
- Check for any household leaks, such as showers, hoses, or taps, and fix them.
- Recycle household items and anything with the recycling label.
- Avoid the use of plastic as much as possible, and switch from plastic bottled water to filtered water.
- Get your friends, family, and others involved with a pledge board.
- Make the switch to digital letters, receipts, and bills, instead of hard copies.

Did You Know…Recent Studies Show…

The trees in the natural forest are declining over the years. You and I, together with strong governance, can protect what is left, and actively plant new trees and bring restoration. While the natural forests act as biodiversity reserves, it keeps carbon, a chemical element, out of oceans and air. It also helps to manage the temperature of the planet, and precipitation. The source of our existence—the air—our today, our tomorrow, and our future, is our responsibility. No trees, no oxygen; no oxygen, no air; no air, no life.

Our animals, on land, sea, and air, are dying out and being more threatened by humans. Whether we are aware of it or not, we are contributing to the loss and destruction of our habitats. We can't afford to lose our species, as they are part of human survival, and deserve to exist. For instance, bees are one of the most important species, as they are necessary for growing food. To prevent loss of biodiversity, you and I, together, can collaborate or partner with local authorities. The protection of wildlife conservation and the restoration of habitats is crucial.

Our soil and land is losing its value due to human activities, like construction, agricultural and industrial activities, and mining. The good news is that we have managed to find ways, such as crop rotation and water-retention, to restore the soil. The challenge is the managing of the soil conservation and passing the restoration techniques to all people in the world and the next generation.

Other environmental issues to consider, which could affect every human and animal on this planet, severely, in the future:

- Air, water, sea, and agricultural pollution
- Climate change and global warming
- Waste disposal and acid rain
- Ozone layer and urban sprawl
- Harmful chemicals and overpopulation

You and I are responsible for the earth like we are for our purpose in life. We are not able to control everything, as change is inevitable, but we can choose to manage what we can. Making a difference does not only apply to people but also to our planet.

You Are Needed

You are a winner when you're not the only one in the spotlight.

I can't remember how old I was—I am guessing between the ages of 21 and 28—but I went through a phase where I could not let go of the thought that there are people, and especially children, in this world who are starving. They don't have access to much or any food, and they go to bed hungry, and live in poverty. How can this be? I questioned myself numerous times. How can one be so deprived from food—one of the basic human needs—and yet there is so much food in this world? Not to mention all the wealth in the world.

I am deeply moved when I turn my focus from myself towards the humanitarian need in our world. There have been many occasions where I have cried—cried because I felt restricted and didn't know how to take the solution further. Sometimes I couldn't help but be frustrated, as I felt my hands were tied. You might be able to relate to what I am saying; however, your frustration might be in a different area. It is not a coincidence that you have that injustice feeling rising up at times.

We were all born to be influencers, to bring solutions to problems. You were born with a creative mind and have the ability to solve problems. When you face hardship yourself, the voice inside you tells you to connect with a friend, family member, or a professional that could help you to get back on your feet. It might not have occurred to you, but your instinct will always tell you to reach out to others for help; it's in you. You can choose to follow that instruction from within, or let it go. There is nothing you can do to take your attachment with people away. None of us would be able to live life without the people in our lives. *Your true life purpose is always connected with others.*

During my teenage years, being one of the toughest times, I tried to figure out ways to do something about poverty. In my head, I had this childlike way of thinking. "I just need a lot of money, but then that wouldn't be enough. Or we, the whole world, could put our money together and feed the poor. We could help them with other facilities and provide them with great resources so that they never have to starve again." I knew that it wasn't a one-man task but a multitude—a collective of people with the same concept, with a rebellious attitude to end poverty. And like what most people do, I buried my drive and passion.

Without a doubt, great things are happening in the world; today, people are more awakened and becoming more aware of disturbing issues: to name only a few, human trafficking, child abduction, poverty, hunger, lack of drinking water, and the spread of infectious diseases. People are actively bringing change, and impacting many lives globally. On the contrary, there is still a lot to do, as there is a large amount of people in the world faced with extreme challenges that none of us could ever imagine going through.

I am aware of the various organizations that are supporting the above-mentioned concerns, and I am thankful for what they are doing. However, it was not until I came across the organization, Global Citizen, where I picked up my passion, hope, and belief again, to live for another worthy cause—ending extreme poverty, by 2030.

"Since 2012, millions of Global Citizens around the world have taken over ten million actions to solve the world's biggest challenges. That's ten million emails, tweets, petition signatures, and phone calls, targeting world leaders to end extreme poverty by 2030."

    Global Citizen is serious in getting our leaders and governments involved together with citizens and other organizations to change our planet and people's lives. Each person deserves to live a high quality life. I truly believe we can only succeed if we get the authorities, the government, and our leaders involved, and influence policies. With their input, we have a better chance to make a difference in our world. This organization believes in the power of unity, and building the world's largest movement for social action to see positive change. Global Citizen is a great platform for you and me—an opportunity, and a chance to impact and to combat some of the world crisis. For more information, go to www.GlobalCitzen.org.

    The world needs you, and while you make yourself valuable, you create a solution using your gift. Your gifts and talents work to serve you and others, and they highlight your place of value in this world. *Discovering your true purpose is making a difference in other people's lives.*

    There are many ways to show your kindness to others and the environment; I encourage you to be creative. All the stories in the previous and this chapter are all great suggestions for you to start and to use it daily, and if you wish, you can pass it onto your friends, family, or strangers. It might feel weird at the beginning, when you start doing it, and that is totally normal. Any new habit can feel uncomfortable at first, but the key is to keep going, and eventually, it will become second nature to you.

"Oprah Winfrey's global influence is unparalleled. Not only has her generosity, and firm belief that education is the key to a better life, benefited countless women and children around the world, but her example has also inspired millions of people to give back in ways big and small."
— Eli Broad

> **Investment Page**
>
> - How important is the environment for you?
> - If anything was possible what part of the world issues would you get involved in?
>
>   Write your answers on the Investment Page.

I am going to share, in the next chapter, the keys for long lasting success; also, how to build a strong *life foundation*, and provide you with small reminders to help you shape your character.

Share Your Investment

Investment Page

_____

_____
_____
_____
_____
_____
_____
_____
_____
_____
_____
_____
_____
_____
_____
_____

CHAPTER 12

Stay a Winner

Like the way a house is built, with a foundation to stand, you would also have to build your own foundation to stand. As earlier mentioned, life comes with many surprises—good and ugly ones—but I believe, if we could get our core right, we would be able to withstand anything that comes our way. I am still learning and still working on my *life foundation*. As humans, we can never outgrow ourselves because it's great to become a better person than the day before. We all have to keep investing in ourselves. I have *Four Ingredients,* which I would like to share with you. My 4 key values for building a strong foundation for my life are the following:

Ingredient 1: The Act of Generosity

True generosity is not a satisfaction for your ego but an act of kindness, to give and to benefit the receiver. You give without asking anything in return, and without counting any cost involved.

I learned at a very early age, from my mother, to be generous to people who I cross paths with. Until today, she still says, "Let your heart be pure, give freely of your love, and be kind to people." Anything you give shall be returned back to you, perhaps not in the same way you gave at first, but rest assured that in some form, it is like the boomerang effect. What you give out is what you receive, and often you actually receive more back than you gave.

Yes, I have been taught to be generous, but that's not why I am generous today. As an adult, I still choose to be generous, and I will tell you why. When I give, it helps me to feel good, because I am helping others, and it makes me happier. There is something special, pleasant, and satisfying about giving what you can to support a person. Practice generosity, and you will experience it for yourself. It will also make you grow as a person, and build great and quality relationships. I say the following humbly, and I am aware that some people find it hard to find great friends.

I consider myself one of the luckiest, as I have amazing, true quality friends that I've known for years. I am surrounded by great friends and consider myself blessed, and no matter where I go, I have no problem making new great friends, because of my generosity.

Before I share how I practice generosity, I would like to say that generosity does not always involve giving money. I had to clarify this because I am aware that some people associate generosity more with finances. Being generous also includes giving your time and energy to others, with enjoyment rather than as an obligation.

Ways I show generosity to friends, family, and strangers:

- Acknowledge people with a smile and a greeting, or by text messaging, and show affection by touching or hugging.
- Give words of encouragement, and give compliments. This is not only something I enjoy and love doing, but I also believe that when you see or think of something great, you should express it; otherwise, it is a waste, don't you think? I am a big believer of positive reinforcement. When you encourage people, it motivates them to do better and sometimes to do more. It also validates their value, and you show respect and appreciation.
- Buy coffee, lunch, or dinner. Buy any small gift that you think will put a smile on someone's face. I will also say, there is no need to wait for a special occasion to buy a small gift for someone; when you feel like it, just do it. It actually makes it more special, as it is an unexpected gift for the receiver.

- I cook extra so I can give some to others.
- Mind children for couples, to give them a date night.
- Last but not least, I love spending quality time with friends and family. We will then take the time for activities such as picnics, going to the beach, or watching movies.

Give yourself the challenge; try some of my recommendations and make a positive change in someone's life. Plus, it will make you feel lighter and happier, and will give you a meaning for your existence.

Don't forget to write your experience of generosity on the Investment Page, after you've tried them.

Ingredient 2: The Act of Gratitude

"Be thankful for what you have, and for what you don't have." You might have heard this statement more than once before, but it is true. Once you understand the importance of that act, you will then know how rich you are. You are rich when you live your life through the act of gratitude. Being thankful about all you see and touch does not only make you a great person, but it also improves your mind to see what's ahead. Moreover, you train yourself to see the good over the bad. The good moments and memories will overpower the bad effects on your subconscious. Gratitude teaches you to use what you have and turn it into something great. Gratitude speaks about your positive attitude and behavior. Saying a simple *thank you* can change someone's view of you, and they will respect you even more. The more you show your appreciation, whether to people or to God, it's a way of paying your highest respect and giving back to the world. The act of gratitude is not only done through words but can also be done through acts of service, gifts, affection, and kindness. Practice gratitude daily, and let it become second nature. You'll see that your days will be much easier, and they will be filled with a positive attitude, regardless what you might be going through. Do not take the act of gratitude lightly; the more positive you are, the more you set yourself up to succeed in life.

How do I do it?

I take the time to write my gratitude in my journal, and also encourage my clients to do the same. The best way to practice the act of gratitude is to say and write down what you are thankful for, daily. You become more aware of your surroundings when you start doing that, and you appreciate how far you have come yourself. You will also realize that you already have a lot to begin with, whether it is friends, family, money, employment, or relationships, or having a range of materialistic goods.

I had the honor to interview leading entrepreneurs, Yvonne Mathews, founder of It's For You, a global business, and Gerry Duffy, founder of Gerry Duffy Academy, and bestselling author and inspirational speaker in personal and professional development. Both share the significance of practicing gratitude; check it out.

Yvonne's Q&A

Why Gratitude?

Why I started to use gratitude...
I feel I have been on a self-discovery journey, from the beginning of the new year, in 2017. I was not happy with my life and felt I needed to start making some big, positive changes in my life. Then I came across the wonderful Tony Robbins, on YouTube, and I started to implement some of the advice he was giving freely. What really resonated with me was that it is almost impossible to feel down or sorry for yourself when you are in a state of appreciation, and the only way to get out of this funk—these bad moods—was to start being grateful, along with some good new habits I adopted. One of these habits was to go for walks along the beach, which basically I had on my door step. I had heard the story of the gratitude rock, so I decided to give it a go. While I was exercising on the beach, I came across a beautiful, small rock, and brought it along with me to the beach. While I was holding the rock in my hand, I started to list all the things I was grateful for—from the runners I was wearing, to the nature that was

around me, and everything I could think of, all the way up to that point in my life. Instantly, I could feel my mood changing; my spirit was getting lifted. I believed that with daily practice, it would bring powerful, positive changes into my life, so I continued. I started to implement the attitude of gratitude!

How long have you been practicing gratitude?

I have been using gratitude for over 17 months now, and there is not one day that goes by where I do not implement it into my day. I started out by using the rock; now I have a notebook, where, every morning, I write down 3–4 sentences of what I am grateful for in my life right NOW. On the opposite page, I write down what I am grateful/thankful for in my future. I call this my gratitude INTENTIONS for the future, where I visualize where I would like to be in the next five years in my personal life and business achievements, and in my overall life in general, as well as where I would like to be living. Not only does my gratitude intentions allow me see where I'm going in my future, but it truly gives me such excitement for where I'm headed, and to know it is possible! I truly believe it begins with being grateful for where you are now, and I believe that better things are coming. It puts me in a happy state.

What do you get out of it?

Practicing gratitude daily really allows me to sit back, take a few minutes, and seriously be thankful for all the incredible opportunities I have experienced throughout my life: to appreciate that I have a roof over my head, food to eat, and clothes to wear, and to not take these things for granted, as so many people in the world do not have these basic things. I find it powerfully shifts my thinking from lack/scarcity—what I feel is missing in my life—to actually focusing on all the positives that I do have; with that comes an instant lift in my mood. When you meditate on it and really be thankful, and not just write for the sake of it, but actually feel it with your heart fully, and be mindful and thankful for what you have, it clears out any negative thoughts. It gives you that extra boost to really stop and think, "Yes, I know I'm not where I want to be, but I will remain focused on where I am going, to really enjoy the journey because, at the end of the day, it is not the destination that makes us happy; it's actually our attitude and our daily habits along the way that lead us to feel contentment, and help us to play out our goals in life."

How has it impacted you on a day-to-day basis, and in your life?

I feel that the world can be a harsh place sometimes. Everywhere you look, people seem to want to share negative stories and sad news. It seems to spread way quicker these days than anything positive. I feel that people sometimes unknowingly focus solely on what's wrong with the world, rather than on what's good in it. So, for that reason, I feel that when I am in a state of appreciation/gratitude, I don't allow it to consume me; I don't allow anything to really phase me anymore. I used to be quite a negative person myself because, everywhere I turned, I would tune into the news, radio, and television, and they all would portray negativity, sad stories, and crimes, which is what seems to sell!

Now, when I hear anything bad, I do not dwell on it, or if someone says something negative, I flip it and try to turn the conversation around. Not only has it helped me in my day-to-day life, and with my mindset, but I feel that whoever I am around can also sense a positive energy, which in turn has a ripple effect on others for the better! If people want to be negative, I don't take it personally; I just bless them and be on my merry way... First thing in the morning, I find myself repeating: Thank You, Thank YOU, THANK YOU—these words, to me, can feel like a prayer, so it does my heart good! I never underestimate the power of gratitude.

Gerry's Q&A

How long have you been practicing gratitude?

I first woke up to this over 25 years ago. I recall, in my early twenties, waiting for several weeks to see a consultant for a very sore throat. In that waiting period, my mind went into overdrive about what might be wrong. I was consumed with worry and was convinced it was something really serious. Such was my enormous relief when he diagnosed something straightforward, I vowed to never forget how lucky I was to get such good news. I think I fell into gratitude almost accidentally because of this incident, as from there, it started to wake me up to what I had, and to what I was so blessed with.

What do you get out of it?

So often, we focus on what we don't have. For me, it's recognizing what we do have.
It helps highlight for me just how wealthy I am in terms of what defines real wealth. With any list of things I am blessed to have, I can always (within seconds) picture someone whom I know who is not as lucky as I am.

How has it impacted you on a day-to-day basis, and in your life?

If I am having a more difficult day, I simply remind myself how much harder it might or would be if I didn't have good health or eyesight, or had pain, like many others are unfortunately given, for whatever reason. I often challenge myself to think of 20 or 50 new things to be grateful for in a day, and it is incredible what an impact it has. Even though I might have something troubling me, I simply ask myself, how much harder would this day be if I didn't have these others things (things are really important). I've long since memorized things I am truly grateful for (arms and legs, great health, living in a great country with resources, infrastructure and opportunities all around, a wonderful group of family and friends, parents who are still alive, etc.). I could list 5,000 other things I've since woken up to as well.

If you have never practiced gratitude before, then I hope I got you excited by introducing you to this technique. Starting from today, train your brain to see what's good and positive, with the practice of gratitude. Take a moment, focus on what you have, and write your gratitude on the Investment Page. It might be uncomfortable at first when you use this technique, but eventually, you will master it. It is a very effective way of retraining your brain.

If you would like ...
To connect with Yvonne, please go to Facebook: @yvonne.mathews.5
To connect with Gerry, please go to www.GerryDuffyAcademy.com

Ingredient 3: The Act of Integrity

"Integrity is doing the right thing, even when no one is watching."

– C.S. Lewis

There are two ways that I look at integrity. First, when speaking to clients on this subject, I use the following analogy:
 If you want to grow apples, or simply have an apple tree in your backyard, you will have to use apple seeds; that's obvious, right? When the time is right, you will see the fruit on the tree, and you will expect to see apples. It is impossible for you to harvest oranges on the apple tree—that would be a crazy surprise, wouldn't you agree? I hope you agree with me that nature will give you what you sow, if the harvest is successful. The lesson here is that you will reap what you sow. Your morals stem from your value; how you set your standards is how you will see things from right and wrong. The question really comes down to, "How much value or respect do you give to a situation?" If it doesn't mean much to you, or you don't respect it as much, sadly, you will not treat it with honesty. Thus, whatever you do,

Stay a Winner

I encourage you to sow with the right attitude, so that when the harvest is ready, you will receive your success in apples, and not be disappointed to receive oranges.

Once, I was working with a client, who came to see me about how she could solve a conflict at her workplace. She had also been told by one of her colleagues that lately, her harsh responses had not been appreciated by the rest of the team.

I asked her, "How honest have you been to yourself recently?"

"What do you mean," she replied.

"Are you experiencing any difficulties at home?"

"What does my private life have to do with my work?" she continued.

"A lot," I said

Looking all confused, she asked, "Why?"

I said, "What's on the inside is what's coming out. How you respond to others is a reflection of what has been playing on the inside. If you hold a grudge, resentment, anger, lack of forgiveness, or bitterness towards someone, and this is not resolved, you carry that with you wherever you go. Unconsciously, you will react towards someone like your colleague—you lashed out with what was sitting deep inside. That uncomfortable feeling and anxiety needs to escape somehow.

It is important to be honest with yourself. Examine yourself, and ask yourself, "Is there anything I am hiding from? And is it worth keeping it that way?" If there are issues that you have not dealt with over the years in your private life, then it is about time for you to do something about it. Keeping things in darkness and not bringing it to the light can hinder you from reaching some of your goals too. This problem will always play in the back of your mind. To set yourself free, you will have to deal with it, and close the door on that subject. Avoiding the problem is what can cause you to react poorly towards others.

You must be aware of what's going on from the inside if the outside is not what you like. Awareness and integrity will enable you to adjust and turn situations around quickly, and to avoid unnecessary conflicts. What is also helpful is to learn to be transparent, and tell or explain to the people around you how you feel at times so that they can give you the space you need. Just remember this: The light always overrules darkness.

Ingredient 4: The Act of Humility

With everyone trying to achieve their goals and dreams, we, as humans, can slip into greed, selfishness, and arrogance. While each of us is trying to make it to the top, we all get smacked down by life. When you least expect it, then you get hit by health problems, a job loss, depression, or financial or relationship problems. Life seems to have its own agenda. Nevertheless—as we touched on earlier—with a positive outlook, setbacks could work out for you in the end. Setbacks are reminders for you and me that we humans are imperfect. During our time of setbacks, we learn, develop, and grow. When we learn to accept an attitude of growth during our trials, we take on humility, and pride fades away. Now, this is priceless, as you then understand that growth means the next level, and the next level means progress, and progress means success.

Humility for me is ….

- Knowing that you had favor along the way to get where you are.
- Knowing that you did not get there by yourself, as others were involved in your journey. You acknowledge and give others the credit for helping you to get to the stage you are at.
- Acknowledging that you don't know everything.
- Developing yourself to become excellent in serving others and thinking of yourself less.

Be humble, and practice humility, and you will gain respect from people.

Stay a Winner

Integrity is keeping your word, doing what you said you will do. And keeping your promises is the most honorable thing you can ever give yourself and others. Being honest and doing the right thing will lead you to success.

You've Got Company

Who is visiting you? Let me just get to the point. Who are you surrounding yourself with? Have you heard of the law of association? It is a well-known fact that you are the average of the 5 people you spend time with. To stay successful, you will have to choose to spend time with the right people. It will not surprise me if you have heard the following statement before: "You become who you hang with." I could not agree more; you must choose your friends wisely. It is important to be around people who will inspire you, especially the ones with ambitions. If you are not an optimistic person, and would like to think positive, then I would say to associate yourself with what you aspire to be. At the end of the day, you want to be around people who are likeminded, or in other words, people who have higher standards than yourself.

Have you ever wondered why it is actually important to associate yourself with the right people? Why do most successful people advise you to spend time with at least five associates who are fruitful in their personal and professional lives?

As simple as it sounds, you either adopt their good or bad habits. Their positive or negative attitude rubs off on you, and you then start to talk, to perceive, to think, and to act like them. It is either that they will encourage and push you to pursue your goals and dreams, or they will hold you back, allowing your setbacks to take over, which can result in not fulfilling your goals and dreams. If you dislike and don't see any positive change or growth in the environment you live in, then perhaps it's time for you to move away. Take the time and think about what you want and who you want to become in the next couple of years. You want friends who hold you accountable, who remind you of your passion, and who will support you to finish what you started. This also applies to your family, and since they are close to you, it's normal for you to expect them to support you. Unfortunately, that's not always the case; you would be surprised how sometimes some family members can pull you back.

In past years, some clients have communicated the insufficient support they received from their family members. As a result, those clients developed self-negative talk.

They would say the following words:

- "I can't do it; I am not worth it."
- "I am never going to make it."
- "I have to be perfect; I am not good enough."

Refuse to allow those words to sink in, if you recognize yourself in this scenario. I can imagine that it's not always easy, but to perform at your best, you will have to step away from the lie. Those negative words are not true. It is sad to know that family members can have a negative impact on you, and perhaps not give you the support you need. So what do you do if you find yourself in similar situation? I then tell my clients to be the role model for their family. I say, "When you are around the family members who don't believe as much in your dream, just be careful when asking them for advice concerning your dream. And any advice given, that doesn't align with your goals, take it with a pinch of salt. Prove to them with your actions, your hard work, optimistic attitude, and positive spirit that your great idea is not impossible. If you know what you want, and you have a clear vision, then you will attract the right people wherever you go. Your vision will dictate who you associate with. And if you are still figuring out what you want, that's also fine. In the meantime, join an association of your interest, and attend seminars, workshops, and conferences. Listening to Podcasts and watching YouTube videos is also a great resource.

Optimistic, ambitious, influential, and successful people don't like to waste their time, and are very much focus-driven. They aim to better themselves by choosing coaches, mentors, great leaders, and influences. They take advice from people who have made a difference in their life and impact others. There is positive fruit for all to witness, and if you like their fruit, ask them how they grew their fruit. That's why it is important to surround yourself with the right people, so you can let them teach and show you how they became successful.

So, don't forget...

- You must first place yourself in the right environment.
- Be around people who dream big, think big, and believe in the impossible.
- Be around people who can improve you.
- Keep developing yourself by joining the right organizations and events.
- Network with people who can help you with your goals and dreams.
- Work harder on yourself, and less on jobs you dislike.
- Prioritize yourself.

Believe in Your Dream

Once, in an interview with Lilian Disney, the interviewer said, "Is it true that Mr. Walt Disney never saw Disneyland?" Lilian answered, "Oh, Mr. Disney saw it; he saw Disneyland way before all of us saw it."

Have you ever wondered why it's hard for other people to believe in your dream? It dawned on me that they never saw or felt the excitement when you first saw your vision or dream. It was only you that saw it! No wonder they can't relate to what you are trying to explain. If they did not see what you saw, how can you blame them for not believing in your idea? Don't lose sleep over it if others don't believe in your ideas. You are the first one to believe that your idea is possible, and that is good enough.

I have no doubt that you have many dreams, but there is always one that stands out more: the one that you keep thinking about and keep creating in your head; the one you are so passionate about that it makes you feel good, it gives you butterflies, and it gets you excited. Sometimes it is so clear that it almost feels real. It almost felt as if you were in that vision; for a second, you felt what it was like to be in the future. The vision or dream was so strong. Could this be your big dream?

Will the world ever see what you see?

Law of Attraction

Before Jim Carry became known as a famous actor, he was broke and had nothing to his name. Apparently, he used to drive every night, park his car at a particular spot, and would visualize things coming to him—things he wanted, like being an actor. He had this insane belief that *"you can manifest anything in your own ability."*

One day, he decided to write a check for 10 million dollars to himself. He dated that check, and kept the check in his wallet for the next 3 years. Amazingly, just before the date that he had initially put, he received the news that he was going to make 10 million dollars for the movie, *Dumb and Dumber.* Jim used the law of attraction to get what he wanted. Over the years, science has experimented that *you can attract what you want* with your faith.

Jim believed in his dream and had already accepted his first check. His faith encouraged him to see the future. Jim once said in an interview, "You get it when you believe you have it."

I was given a memorable gift for my birthday, by an amazingly good friend, who strongly believes in the principle of the law of attraction. To keep the excitement for me, and not to get off course during the process of writing this book, she gave me a special pen. As an encouragement, I mean to use this pen for signing this book for you at one of my book launches. If you have not seen my special pen yet, go to www.ExchangeAndWinLife.com to see the full-sized, colored picture.

Getting what you want starts with your faith. The law of attraction becomes essential if you want to keep the dream alive. You must keep yourself focused and create a little evidence, or something tangible for yourself, like Jim and myself.

Your Words Are Powerful

You are the master of your own life.

Did you know that your words are very powerful? While you use the law of attraction, together with your faith, you will also have to watch how you speak. There is a vigorous connection between your mind and your spoken word. Your brain creates your words, your mind helps you think and manage your words, and you then decide to speak what you thought. Every time you speak, you reinforce your mind to believe what you say. If you want to have positive thoughts, or you are training your mind to think positively, you must help yourself and speak only words of affirmation. What you say is what you end up believing. What you believe is what you will follow; what you follow is what you will act upon. What you act upon, or do, is your outcome. Your outcome is what you manifested and gave birth to when you initially spoke. For instance, if you keep saying to yourself you can't walk 5 kilometers, you end up believing that you can never walk 5 kilometers. If you change that around and say, "I can walk 5 kilometers," you will believe that too. The major difference is that positive thinking automatically encourages you to find a plan to achieve the goal. Negative thinking tells you that you don't have to reach 5 kilometers and, therefore, you end up doing nothing. Understand that your words are powerful; therefore, be mindful of how you speak. How you speak affects everything and dictates your decisions and how you perceive life. Be aware of your negative self-talk, and replace it with sentences like the following:

- I am healthy.
- I am successful.
- I am the best in what I do.
- I will accomplish…by the year….
- I can do…and I'm not going to let…stop me.
- I have found my purpose and know what I am meant to be doing.
- I know that…is possible.

These are just examples. I want you to take the time to write some positive words of affirmation on the Investment Page.

Treat Yourself!

I take really good care of something that is precious, costly or expensive and especially when it's new. I maintain it, keep it in good shape, give it extra attention and do not lose sight of it. In the same way, that's how I view myself—a highly regarded, exclusive person—and I love to give myself the best treatment. By all means you are also exceptional—a winner— and worthy, an extravagant individual. Give yourself *first* class treatment, be open to give yourself the best, and know that you are loved by at least one person. Set your standards; your worth cannot be compared with anything or anyone. You might ask, "But Cynthia, how do I select myself as premium?" There are many things you can do to gain more confidence and boost your high self-esteem. I have chosen some of my favorites for you: The Top Ten—Triple T or 3T, which will help you keep your self-esteem up.

Do something positive for yourself everyday. This could be anything from something you enjoy to a challenge you have never done before which includes other people. The result of doing ONE beneficial activity everyday will produce and enhance your *feel* good emotions.

Give yourself the best breakfast lunch, dinner, and dessert. It's important that you eat healthy and take care of your body. You have been given only one body, and that has to go a long way. Caring about yourself is to respect, love, and to take care of your health.

Stay a Winner

Exercise! Now this could be indoors and outdoors. If you're someone like me, you could go for walks on the beach, go to parks, go hiking, or just go for a run in the neighborhood. You can join a sports club that organizes sports games and activities, or you can hit the gym.

Sign up for self development activities, or any other course. An ongoing self-education is not only a great way to exercise your brain and gain knowledge, but it can also boost your self-confidence and self-esteem. At the same time, you are interacting with other people, psychologically and mentally, and this adds positivity to your sanity.

Spend quality time with friends and family. You heard me— Quality, not Quantity. Take the time to give your time. Allow your loved ones to experience the best of you. There is more gained when time is not rushed.

Have the mindset of always choosing the best places, items, presents, clothes, shoes, accessories, restaurants, bars,cafes, foods, holidays, books, music...you get the idea. The question is, "Why would you NOT pick the best from what is available to you?"

Get out of your comfort zone and explore what's around you. Visit places, cities and countries you have never been before, and take a companion with you if you need one.

Be open, get to know or acknowledge a person and people around you. See the best in them. Saying hello does not cost you anything, so be nice; greet someone and put a smile on their face. It's as simple as that!

Taste! Experience something that you have never tried before.

Be open to try various cultural dishes but also make sure to eat more organic foods over processed foods. The more natural colors on your plate, the more appealing it is to the eyes and the healthier it is for you. Eating healthy and the right type of food will boost your vitality and energy. Your body, skin and hair will glow and you will feel great inside. And when you feel healthy you tend to be more productive and make better decisions.

Oh, and don't forget to drink plenty of Water!

Think big, and do not limit yourself or sell yourself too short.

Life has more to offer you—more than you can possibly think, ask or imagine.

Challenge yourself, and be creative in every possible way in all areas of your life.

To live a prosperous life, spend more time on yourself. Use your gifts and talents, and turn your focus towards others.

*If you would like to receive your FREE Triple T copy go to www.ExchangeAndWinLife.com and simply download your full size print ready version.

Investment Page

- Like Walt, what do you see? How much do you believe in your dream, and what are you going to do about it?
- How are you going to manifest your Law of Attraction? And when you discover it, please tell me your story.

Write your answers on the Investment Page.

Are you ready to boost your self-esteem? You better be! I didn't want to leave you without highlighting how incredible you are. Turn the page for the next chapter.

Investment Page

CHAPTER 13

Leave Your Mark

You don't decide to become a victim,
but you can decide to become a victor.

    Do you remember, in Chapter 10, when I spoke about the special person who had passed away? I wonder who you guessed. It was Comfort, my biological mother.
    Comfort's life has taught me some serious lessons. No one decides to become a victim; and therefore, it has never been, and it is not, your fault. Meanwhile, what you can do is decide to become a victor. If this is you, then be encouraged: although it might feel as if you don't have a choice, I want to tell you that you have a choice. You can choose to overcome, and you don't need to replay the past in your mind. Comfort fell into *the victim trap* of victimization. Once more, you can overcome anything, and it is all possible. Don't give up on yourself; it's not over until you say it's over. No matter how bad things look, hold on and don't let go; you are going to be fine. You are a fighter like me! Use your setbacks as a stepping stone to get where you want to be in life.

> **Investment Page**
>
> Please take a moment and reflect on the following if this applies to you.
>
> - Have you become a victim in your life?
> - Have you allowed your past to interfere with your future goals and where you want to go?
> - Are you a victor today, not allowing anything in your life to stop you from becoming who you want to become?
>
> Please write your thoughts on the Investment Page or in your notebook.

You Were Born a Winner

"Always be yourself, express yourself, and have faith in yourself; do not go out and look for a successful personality and duplicate it."
— Bruce Lee

I want you to read this slowly and believe in the following words: You are born a winner.

Who you are is perfect; the way you look is perfect; the way you walk is perfect; the way your voice sounds is perfect. The way you were created was perfect. You are perfect for what you were born to do. You are an original; you never want to be someone else—the world needs YOU. You matter, and as long as you have not fulfilled all your potential, without your gift, something is missing on this earth. Do not hide your personality behind others but be yourself. Give yourself the approval for who you are, and don't let anyone do that for you.

You are a winner.

Everything you are supposed to do on this earth is waiting for you, and it all depends on you. As long as you believe, everything you could imagine or think of is possible. Nothing will happen, come to pass, or be fulfilled, until you activate your potential. The key is that you don't wait for opportunities; you go out and create them.

You are unique.

Be In Competition With Yourself—Do You

You stand out when you are yourself.

Are you satisfied with where you are, or is there more? Are you happy or content with what you have achieved so far?

I hope your answer is no. I am going to assume you said no. It is *no,* because you want to achieve more, as there is more.

It is already within you to look ahead and see how you can achieve more. The challenge is, how far will you go? When you are ready to move forward, anything is possible, and nothing can stop you from achieving great and honorable things. Success follows the act of service and kindness; it is impossible for you not to receive anything in return. You will receive your reward from working hard, persevering, and disciplining yourself.

 Be in competition with yourself and focus on yourself only. Challenge yourself with what you did yesterday, last week, last month, last year, and the years before. **Don't worry about what others are doing, but let their work inspire you to become a better you.**

Be reminded that each of us has a responsibility to maximize ourselves and use our potential to the fullest. If that's the case, then understand that there is no need for you to be in competition with others. We are supposed to be exchanging our values with one another, so that each and every one of us can benefit from one another.

"Comparison is a thief of joy." – Theodore Roosevelt
Don't compare yourself to anyone.

Aim to live an extraordinary life on your own terms. You don't want to look back in 2, 3, or 5 years' time, with regret. Imagine if you did not change much, or you only made some few unhappy changes in your life. If you start today, your regrets for the future are reduced. It's never too late to start anything, regardless of your age. Remember Colonel, founder of KFC; for him, it was at the age of 66. It is better to start today than never.

Only focus on YOU.

True Success for YOU is…

"Try not to become a man of success, but rather try to become a man of value."
– Albert Einstein

True success for you is…
Knowing who you are and why you are here, and what you are meant to be doing. You measure success by your own ability—what you can do, your potential, and talent—within your reach. You should never measure success by comparing yourself to others around you. You are successful if you are doing what you were created for; this includes sharing your gift with others.

I have a small exercise for you. If we have to measure success, which of the following do you think is *true success?*

A. Let's say you like playing piano, and you have been taking lessons since you were 7 years old, but you stopped practicing at 18. You are now 26 years old, you have a day job in the corporate sector, and you only play piano at family gatherings. Music, and especially piano, is still your passion, however it looks like you will be working at your office job for the next 5 years.

B. Imagine you are playing piano, have concerts, and are traveling to different countries to play, and you also have a distinct way of playing the piano, which differs from all the other pianists.

C. Assuming you work in a music store during the week, you play piano casually, and randomly, on some weekends. Any gig you can get your hands on, you take it.

Here is my take on the scenarios:

A: Sadly, you are not doing what you truly want; you are not following your passion.
B: To me, this is true success, because you have utilized your gift to the maximum, and you continue to bless others with it. You are following your passion.
C: You are on the right path to fulfill your success dream. Additionally, with hard work, creativity, and setting yourself apart, you will inspire others and reach your full potential.

As I mentioned earlier, modern research have shown that wealth, fame, or power can't give you true happiness. It is important to do the following if you want to live a happy life: Keep yourself focused, and don't seek financial success first, but seek to become who you're meant to be—the original. Once you discover what you are meant to be doing, your financial success will automatically follow you. Who you are and what you do is what will define you. You are powerful beyond measure, and capable of doing anything you want. You were born as an influencer. Once you understand your strengths, value, who you truly are, and what you are meant to be doing for others, everything inside you will tell you to go after what you feel. Success will come to you. You don't have to chase success; if you develop your gift, people will remember you. Like Steve Jobs said, *"Follow your passion first, and the money will come after."*

Success must first start with your purpose.

You Are Making a Difference

Be encouraged that making a difference does not mean you have to change the world. Only focus on one or a few people in your community, like Nick Vujicic's story, and before you know it, you will be impacting many. Understand that when you take the time to reach out to a person, you empower them to do the same. They might not help another person in the same way that you did, but they will understand the principle of turning their focus from themselves, and seeing the need in another person.

I want to challenge you to leave your legacy, at least with your friends, family, and community. Start there, and you will see what happens. You probably won't understand what a blessing it is to change someone's world until you have tried it yourself. It is infectious! I promise you; you will see a ripple effect as each of us starts reaching out by using our gifts and talents—using what we have. You become extensive and inspiring to those around you. People will remember you when you inspire them. Don't underestimate who you are and what difference you can make.

I want to make a difference in your life, not only by giving you this book but also with the letters **X** and **W**. You might wonder why the letter **X** and **W** are in blue in the title of this book. I was asked by friends and family, "Why are the letters **X** and **W** in blue? Does it mean anything?" Well, just be warned that it will stick with you forever once you know the thought behind the letters. So don't blame me!

My reason for making the letters stand out is for *you*; your *life* matters to me. You are meant to see the letters as a logo or a sign for you to exchange your gift with the world. I want you to remember the following:

The letter **X** is what I call the *check in with yourself* letter. It is not common, not a regular letter, and you will not come across it as often as the **W**. But when you spot the **X,** I want you to ask yourself the following:

- "Am I doing what I love?"
- "Am I currently using my gifts to serve others?"
- "Am I on the creativity path—planning my success?"

Every time you see the **W**, be reminded that you were born a WINNER. You are a winner because you have something to offer— your value. You have greatness in you!

Each person is meant to impact, help, influence, and make a difference in someone's life.

Please share your stories with me, and let me know how this book has impacted you and your life.

Go to www.ExchangeAndWinLife.com for emailing
Instagram: CynthiaTheAuthor
Facebook: @cynthia.asante.12
 Twitter   : CynthiaAsante6

I Believe in YOU

Together, we have come this far. We touched on setbacks: delays or hindrances, small and large life challenges that are sometimes beyond our control; a situation where you feel stuck or inadequate. Yet, with time, it helps you to get stronger, and it permits us to comfort others; it gives us a license to improve, and to teach about our mistakes and our victories in life.

If it wasn't for God, I wouldn't be where I am today. The Bible helped me to answer some of the most challenging yet simple questions in life. When things were not easy, and when no one was there to hold me or to tell me that things were going to be okay, it was through my faith in God that I was able to stand on my feet.

I want you to listen carefully: I believe in you, and I mean it when I say that. I believe in you because there is nothing you are not able to perform or can become. You have been given everything you need, and you are not short of anything. If I can pursue my dreams, so can you.

I have two *"Do Not's"* for you:

1. Do Not let someone who gave up on their dreams talk you out of yours.
2. Do Not live to exit; you are worth more than that. If anything, I love what Dr. Myles Munroe once said, *"The goal for your future is to make history. The next generation should read about you."* You are born to inspire others around you. Together, we are created for one another. No one is meant to be left out, so don't choose to do so but go forward and shine. Exchange your value with another person and the rest of the world. Do not sell yourself too short, embrace possibility, and go after what you truly want. As long as you and I are breathing, there is still much left in us, and more to exchange with others.

Your talents and gifts are *your* gems, and your character and personality aren't to be compared with any other precious stones. Your appearance is a masterpiece and, therefore, your presence is an ornament to the world. Permit yourself to shine, excel, and grow, with a progressive, positive mindset, and to become a high valued person.

Involve others in your journey, and allow them to get the best out of you. I didn't get to the stage I am at today by myself. I had others supporting, encouraging, and cheering me on to get where I am now. Even with this book, I had coaches, friends, colleagues, and families helping me to put it together.

We need one another; you can't get there by yourself, so give your best to receive the best.

One thing I note, which most successful people have in common, is that they model an act of service through their gifts and talents; this is their way of giving back to the world.

Focus on you, be in competition with yourself, and stay positive. Become the best you!

See old things in a different way. Don't think too small of yourself, as you are needed! I hope I have shifted your perspective and you are excited for what's ahead of you. I am thrilled to see you live the life you always wanted. I know you'll shine wherever you go, while you follow your dreams make sure you include me. I really would love to know how this book has impacted you. So get in touch with me at www.ExchangeAndWinLife.com.

I want to leave you with this thought: *"Design, Plan, Act, and Believe Your Success is Inevitable*—so go get what's yours."

Find your purpose in life.
Give your best to receive the best.
Make your decisions based on your vision.

Investment Page

RECAP

Let's do a recap and put everything together.

To make your life easier, I have provided a summary of all the main concepts and principles from each chapter, for you to return to, anytime you wish.

Chapter 1
- Recognize your value and sense of worth
- Become aware of the world we live in and what we have been educating on

Chapter 2
- You must take responsibility for your future
- Make a decision that quitting is not an option
- Setbacks are only distracters and, therefore, they can work in your favor

Chapter 3
- You have more strength in you than you realize
- How to control your emotions and your mind
- Take time to renew your mind and make room for creative ideas

Chapter 4
- How to turn your focus from yourself and benefit from it
- Stay true to your identity and don't change YOU for anyone

Chapter 5
- Set yourself free, leave the comfort zone and follow your instinct
- The importance of your purpose, potential, vision, dreams, and gifts
- How to say no, and love what only matters to you

Chapter 6
- Look to others who have succeeded, and motivate yourself into action
- Believe you can fulfill your dreams too

Chapter 7
- Why it is important to have a vision
- Use what you've got to prosper
- How to take yourself to the next level

Chapter 8
- Apply the 5 senses tool kit

Chapter 9
- How to plan your success
- How to become financially successful

Chapter 10
- Invest in a life of giving
- The importance of looking beyond yourself
- 7 key concepts on the act of service and kindness

Chapter 11
- How to make a difference globally
- Looking after the planet is also a way of turning your focus from yourself

Chapter 12
- Practice generosity, gratitude, integrity, and humility
- How to prioritize the right people for your dream journey
- The power of your imagination and words
- Embrace the best that life has to offer you – Triple T

Chapter 13
- Leave your long lasting legacy
- You can become or do anything your heart desires

About the Author

Cynthia Asante was born in Accra, Ghana; at age 5, she moved to the Netherlands. She moved to Australia at age 23, and straight after that, she graduated from college. She completed her bachelor's degree in Commerce and Theology, and her postgraduate in Counseling, and started her own private practice in Sydney. As a professional Counselor and Behavioral Therapist, in the past 15 years, Cynthia has helped, changed, and impacted individuals, young and old, from all walks of life. She has an infectious enthusiasm and passion to see people's lives change, and creates an awareness of one's value. Her contagious approach to positive reinforcement continues to touch people's lives in deep and profound ways. This positive vibe has inspired many to pursue their own purpose in life, and to discover their full potential. Inspired by the land of saints and scholars, Cynthia decided, in 2017, to live in Dublin, Ireland, to fulfill her childhood dream: publishing her first of many books to come. Cynthia lives between both countries, Ireland and Australia.

Book Cynthia to Speak

If you would like Cynthia as your keynote speaker, coach, or a guest at your event/ seminar, please get in touch directly here, at www.ExchangeAndWinLife.com.

Cynthia is also available for delivering educational talks at your school, university, and startup businesses.

Exchange Setbacks for Winning

To order more books, please go to:
www.amazon.com
www.ExchangeAndWinLife.com
Also available in all major bookshops

    I hope this book has changed some of your old mindset, and you are now influenced to work on your own dreams. If you were inspired by this book, please give, lend, or pass this copy onto someone who might need it. Or, if you wish, buy them their own copy for their birthday, Christmas, graduation gift, or any special occasion. There is nothing better in life than to bless, help another person, and to see them exceed beyond their own expectation.

    Please share your stories with me, and let me know how this book has impacted you and your life.

Go to www.ExchangeAndWinLife.com for emailing
Instagram: CynthiaTheAuthor
Facebook: @cynthia.asante.12
Twitter: CynthiaAsante6

www.ingramcontent.com/pod-product-compliance
Lightning Source LLC
Chambersburg PA
CBHW072130160426
43197CB00012B/2057